UPRISING

ALSO BY JOHN NICHOLS

It's the Media, Stupid
(with Robert W. McChesney, 2000)

*Jews for Buchanan: Did You Hear the One About
the Theft of the American Presidency?* (2001)

Our Media, Not Theirs
(with Robert W. McChesney, 2002)

Dick: The Man Who Is President (2004)

Against the Beast: An Anti-Imperialist Reader (editor, 2004)

*Tragedy & Farce: How the American Media Sell Wars,
Spin Elections, and Destroy Democracy*
(with Robert W. McChesney, 2005)

The Genius of Impeachment (2006)

*The Death and Life of American Journalism:
The Media Revolution That Will Begin the World Again*
(with Robert W. McChesney, 2010)

*The "S" Word:
A Short History of an American Tradition: Socialism* (2011)

UPRISING

How Wisconsin Renewed
the Politics of Protest,
from Madison to Wall Street

John Nichols

NATION
BOOKS

New York

Published by Nation Books,
A Member of the Perseus Books Group
116 East 16th Street, 8th Floor
New York, NY 10003
www.nationbooks.org

Nation Books is a co-publishing venture of
the Nation Institute and the Perseus Books Group

Books published by Nation Books are available at special discounts for
bulk purchases in the United States by corporations, institutions, and other
organizations. For more information, please contact the Special Markets
Department at the Perseus Books Group, 2300 Chestnut Street, Suite 200,
Philadelphia, PA 19103, or call (800) 810-4145, ext. 5000,
or e-mail special.markets@perseusbooks.com.

Editorial production by Marrathon Production Services. www.marrathon.net

DESIGN BY JANE RAESE
Text set in 12-point Bembo

A CIP catalog record for this book is available from the Library of Congress.

ISBN 978-1-56858-703-5
ISBN 978-1-56858-706-6 (e-Book)

3 5 7 9 10 8 6 4 2

FOR HARRISON WOOD NICHOLS,

a descendent of Abner Nichols,
the Cornish tin miner who came in 1824
to mine lead at Mineral Point, Wisconsin

CONTENTS

CONTENTS

FOREWORD

But that desire is still out there. It's the force behind a
huge new movement we don't even have a name for yet,
a movement that's not a left opposed to a right, but perhaps a below against above, little against big, local and
decentralized against consolidated. If we could throw out
the old definitions, we could recognize where the new
alliances lie; and those alliances—of small farmers, of factory workers, of environmentalists, of the poor, of the
indigenous, of the just, of the farseeing—could be ex-
traordinarily powerful against the forces of corporate
profit and institutional violence.
                —Rebecca Solnit, "Acts of Hope," 2004

WHEN THE Fox News channel's Bill O'Reilly reported
on a supposed outbreak of "union thug" violence during the mass protests that erupted in Wisconsin in the winter
of 2011, Rupert Murdoch's network coupled its report of al-
leged thuggery in Madison with images of men pushing and
shoving another in front of palm trees.
    Palm trees are not native to Wisconsin.
    But they are useful for the purposes of this book.

Fox claims to offer a news report that is "fair and balanced." And if that is the fantasy you prefer, then I am certain Mr. O'Reilly will be pleased to provide it.

This book, on the other hand, rejects the fantasy.

I am not an unbiased observer, and this is not an unbiased account.

How could I be? I am a Wisconsinite. I was proud of my state before it became the westernmost exemplar of the Arab Spring, before its name became synonymous with the term "uprising," before plastic cheeseheads became political statements so infused with meaning that in the fall of 2011, "Occupy Wall Street" protesters erupted with cheers at the arrival of allies adorned with the cheddar.

I was born and raised in Wisconsin. So was my mother, and my father. So were my grandparents on both sides. And my great-grandparents. And my great-great-grandparents. My relatives on my mother's side and my father's side settled in Wisconsin before statehood. I've got a relative, living or dead, in every crossroads town from Green Bay to Grant County, from Mineral Point to Madison, from Owen to Oshkosh.

I was raised in southeastern Wisconsin, just west of Racine and Kenosha, in a place and time when unions were honorable and omnipresent. I met Teddy Kennedy at the United Auto Workers Local 72 hall in Kenosha, read the Racine labor newspaper even before my friend Roger Bybee became the editor, and never entertained the notion that any politician, Republican or Democrat, would dare to try and break a union.

When I finished graduate school, I turned down an offer to work for a nonunion paper in Pennsylvania and hired on as a reporter for the *Blade* in Toledo, Ohio. The day I arrived, I proudly signed my card as a member of the Newspaper Guild, AFL-CIO. I was "union" then, and I'm "union" now.

That's where I come from, and that's where this book comes from.

I thought Wisconsin mattered before my old friend Scott Walker—yes, the governor and I were once on good terms—tried to strip away the collective bargaining rights of state, county, and municipal employees and my kid's first-grade teacher, Susan Stern. I thought it mattered even more after my neighbors David Panofsky and Pat Smith, my high school pal Marcia Vlach, my mom's friends from Burlington and Union Grove, and a hundred thousand or so other Wisconsinites showed up with their handmade signs at the capitol and kicked off the most remarkable labor uprising in modern American history.

This book examines that uprising from a number of perspectives, not merely to offer a sense of what happened and what is still happening in Wisconsin but to consider what an uprising and its aftermath may mean for labor, for popular organizing, for media reform, for politics, for democracy. And, perhaps most important, how one uprising inspires the next.

The chapters are organized around themes, rather than along a timeline. Some of the same people show up in multiple chapters, a few stories are retold, from slightly different angles to make slightly different points. And some touchstones, the wisdom of Tom Paine and Walt Whitman, the groundbreaking insights of my friend and inspiration Howard Zinn and his true successor, Rebecca Solnit, are omnipresent. So, too, is Naomi Klein, who explained the "shock doctrine" that was so very much on display in Wisconsin's budget fight. The mashup will come as no surprise to anyone who witnessed the remarkable events that played out in Wisconsin. Traditional boundaries were crossed, again and again and again. Students became leaders. Legislators became outlaws. Union leaders became media producers. Musicians became organizers. Sheriff's deputies became protesters. Librarians announced that they were not afraid of the National Guard. And Republican legislators made a mockery of the Constitution they claimed to cherish with something akin to biblical reverence. "Wisconsin" was, and is, a whirlwind. And it has swept far beyond the borders of one state, which is why this book references and celebrates struggles from Cairo to Kalamazoo, from Ohio's successful campaign to overturn that state's anti-labor law to the movement that decided to "Occupy Wall Street."

There are heroes who go unmentioned, and I regret that. I regret not having the space to recount every brilliant, bold, and hilarious slogan on every sign at every march, although I do hope folks will recall the one attached by an eighty-year-old woman to the device she used to keep her balance: AT LEAST THIS WALKER IS USEFUL. I regret not having the space to name every brilliant, bold, and hilarious Wisconsinite who held those signs, "come rain or sleet or dark of night—come wind or frigid snow," as Tom Morello sang in his song of the Wisconsin struggle, "Union Town." But I do want to mention a few people who made this book possible. The editors at the *Nation*, including Katrina vanden Heuvel, Roane Carey, Richard Kim, Betsy Reed, Emily Douglas, Frank Reynolds, Peter Rothberg, Gennady Kolker, my fellow reporters and writers, the interns, the web team. Everyone recognized the importance of what was playing out in Wisconsin and nationally. They supported and sustained my reporting, as did Dave Zweifel, Paul Fanlund, Chris Murphy, and especially Lynn Danielson and the amazing Judie Kleinmaier of the *Capital Times*. I am a media critic by training and avocation, which makes me all the more proud of the role that the *Capital Times* and the *Nation* played in telling the story of Wisconsin and in providing perspective on how and why it mattered.

The reporting and commentary contained in this book comes from the coverage I did for the *Nation* and the *Capital Times,* as well as from pieces I wrote for the *Progressive* magazine (a hey to Matt Rothschild, Ruth Conniff, and Amitabh Pal) and the *Guardian.* The ideas were shaped and honed in repeated appearances on radio programs hosted by John "Sly" Sylvester, Mitch Jeserich, Suzi Weissman, Thom Hartmann, Ed Schultz, Laura Flanders, and the heroic Amy Goodman. I was pleased to be a frequent guest on Ed Schultz's MSNBC program, as well as the other shows on that network; I am especially grateful to Ed and James Holm, as well as Rich Stockwell, Gregg Cockrell, Arianna Jones, Sheara Braun and the rest of the crew. I developed many of the ideas in presentations to organizations across the country, including Free Press, the media reform group that Bob McChesney and I formed with Josh Silver some years ago. Craig Aaron, Tim Karr, and other folks at Free Press invited me to use the 2011 National Conference for Media Reform to begin to address the communications issues that were rising in the states, and I truly appreciate that, as I do the opportunities that the Sheet Metal Workers, National Nurses United, the American Federation of Teachers, the International Labor Communications Association, the Sidney Hillman Foundation, the Left Forum, the International Federation of Journalists, We Are Wisconsin, Fighting Bob Fest, Burlington Area Progressives, Ithaca College, and so many other unions, organizations, and schools gave me to develop the narratives that underpin this book.

John Matthews, Peter Rickman, Bruce Colburn, Mary Bell, Bryan Kennedy, Art Foeste, Phil Neuenfeldt, Marty Beil, Mahlon Mitchell, Leo Gerard, Randi Weingarten, Rose Ann

DeMoro, and a thousand other heroes from every corner of the union movement, and the social-justice movements that align and affiliate with organized labor (hey there, Scott Goodstein) were, and are, remarkably wise and generous sources. And the same goes for political players such as Bernie Sanders, Russ Feingold, Keith Ellison, Dennis Kucinich, Marcy Kaptur, Tammy Baldwin, Gwen Moore, Dale Schultz, Mark Miller, Lena Taylor, Fred Risser, Jon Erpenbach, Paul Soglin, Dave Mahoney, Mark Pocan, Corey Mason, Doug LaFollette, and so many others. (I even have to thank Scott Walker here, not for his policies, but for many conversations in the better days when he was more interested in the rich and freewheeling debates of Wisconsin than in the sweet nothings whispered by billionaires on the phone.)

Mary Bottari, who turns up in several chapters of this book, is truly a better half and an endless source of insight, information, and wisdom. Whitman Bottari keeps me focused on the fights that matter most, and she sure knows how to use a bullhorn. (Her teachers, Mary Jo Yttri and Susan Stern, were and are heroes of the struggle and heroes of the classroom; and we couldn't have done it without Whitman's hero, Oma Vic McMurray.) My mother, Mary Nichols, and my father, Harrison Wood Nichols, made me a Wisconsinite. My sister Cary went above and beyond the call of duty in 2011, which is her nature. And I kept getting these lovely emails from my sister Kitty, who suddenly became quite political.

No one ever had a finer friend or cowriter than Bob McChesney, who provided expert analysis, cheered me on, and waited patiently as our joint projects were delayed. And I love our Wisconsinites-in-exile, especially my friend from childhood and cheesehead champion, Mark Janson. I live in a community that provides constant support and encouragement and

FOREWORD

I thank David Panofsky, Pat Smith, Nikki Anderson, Lee Cullen, Sharon Lezberg, Brian Yandell, Marc Scateni, Susannah Peterson, Laura Dresser, Joel Rogers, Ed Garvey, John Matthews, Paul and Mari Jo Buhle, Allen Ruff, Inger Stole, and the Lapham parents. I'm indebted to Marsha Rummel and the folks at Rainbow Bookstore Co-op and the baristas at Ancora Coffee Roasters. And I won't soon forget tooling around Wisconsin with Thomas Frank, who immortalized my hometown of Union Grove.

Carl Bromley made this book possible with just the right combination of patience and prodding. I value him as an editor and a friend. And the same goes for John Sherer, Dori Gelb, Ruth Baldwin, Christine Marra, and everyone else who embraced this project.

Uprising is dedicated to my father—and to Terry Fritter, Patty Allen, Marv Vike, Ed Sadlowski Jr., Sly, and the Winter Soldiers.

What is it that is swelling the ranks of the dissatisfied? Is it a growing conviction in state after state, that we are fast being dominated by forces that thwart the will of the people and menace representative government?

—Robert M. La Follette,
July 4, 1897, Mineral Point, Wisconsin

CHAPTER 1

"Madison, Wisconsin, Let's Get Rowdy!"

On the Cold First Night of a Golden Age

I speak the password primeval, I give the sign of
democracy!
—Walt Whitman, *Leaves of Grass*, 1855

To Our Friends in Madison, Wisconsin: I wish you could
see firsthand the change we have made here. Justice is
beautiful, but justice is never free. The beauty of Tahrir
Square you can have everywhere, on any corner, in any
city, or in your heart. So hold on tightly and don't let go.
. . . Breathe deep, Wisconsin, because justice is in the air.
And may the spirit of Tahrir Square be in every beating
heart in Madison today.
—letter from Egyptian activist Maor Eletrebi,
read by Tom Morello, February 21, 2011

I THOUGHT CAIRO WOULD BE WARMER
—protest sign, Madison, Wisconsin, February 2011

Hɪsᴛᴏʀʏ ᴅᴏᴇsɴ'ᴛ happen on schedule. It comes at you, sometimes when you least expect.

Sometimes on a very cold, very windy Monday night in February, a few blocks from a state capitol where crooked politicians are conniving to take away the essential rights of working people, sometimes in a cavernous room packed with high school and college students, a band takes a stage from one side of an epic tipping point and leaves on another, having bent the arc of history in a moment so fast, so furious, so unexpected that it is too easy to tell yourself you are just imagining all of this. And then reality kicks in. You can see it, you can hear, you can touch it; what's all around you matters more than anything you have ever experienced because you realize that you are not waiting for the future anymore. You are in it.

I have covered great wars. I have covered epic elections. I have hiked the mountains of El Salvador with peasant rebels. I have crossed Middle Eastern borders under cover of darkness. I have pondered threats to civil liberties with the libertarian scholars of the Cato Institute, and threats to economic liberties with the last of the Reuther brothers. I have dined with George Herbert Walker Bush on white linen-covered tables at the White House and I have grabbed Mexican food with Bill Clinton on the night before his first election. I have joked with George W. Bush, challenged Dick Cheney, and prodded Barack Obama. I have driven with Paul Wellstone down country roads to stand in solidarity with farmers fighting foreclosure. I have walked with Nelson Mandela on the Cape Flats. I have been around a good bit of history. But nothing prepared me for the night of February 21, 2011.

The state of my birth was one week into an epic uprising that would capture of the attention of the nation and then the world, inspiring similar protests in states across the United States and finally in the shadows of Wall Street skyscrapers. The uprising of February and March 2011 would make a single word, "Wisconsin," not just the name of a state but the reference point for a renewal of labor militancy, mass protest, and radical politics.

Governor Scott Walker, a Republican narrowly elected three months earlier in the Republican sweep of November 2010, was proposing to strip state, county, and municipal employees, as well as teachers in public schools, technical colleges, and universities, of the collective bargaining rights and the union representation that provide the last thin layers of protection for working people in an era of globalization, privatization, downsizing, and deep cuts, and that add a few popular voices to a politics where money speaks and corporations shout.

The governor had everything he needed to make his move. A recent election victory sufficient to claim a mandate. Control of both houses of the state legislature. Dysfunctional Democratic opposition. A think tank, right-wing talk radio, direct mail and messaging machine funded by billionaire backers such as Charles and David Koch. A pliant press that swallowed spin about "overpaid" public employees and "overwhelming" budget deficits as if it was mother's milk. And unions already so battered by the demands for cuts, givebacks, and furloughs from a supposedly friendly previous Democratic administration that they were reeling even before they took the hit.

Defeating the agenda of a particularly reactionary governor in Wisconsin and of a broader right-wing project to which that governor had pledged his allegiance was not just a daunting task. It was, by the estimate of most pundits and politicos, even those who sympathized with the workers and their unions, a hopeless struggle destined to fail so ingloriously that talk of mounting even the most rudimentary challenge was commonly dismissed as a fool's mission. But someone forgot to tell the students. On the day after Walker announced his plan, having been called to action by union activists who declared that "what we do in the next five days will determine whether we keep our union, and our professional lives as educators, researchers and public servants," fifty members of the Teaching Assistants' Association at the University of Wisconsin—the oldest union of graduate employees in the world—gathered in front of the Memorial Union on their campus and raised handmade signs and teeth-chattering voices in protest.

Two days later, they gathered again and marched, more than a thousand strong, to the capitol. And they kept marching, joined by members of other embattled public-sector unions, and then by members of private-sector unions who recognized that their rights were threatened as well, then by retirees and high school students, by farmers and small-business owners. The numbers grew each day, to five thousand, to ten thousand, to twenty thousand, to fifty thousand, to a hundred thousand just one week after that first rally by the teaching assistants. The capitol was surrounded and then peacefully occupied by thousands of teachers, snowplow drivers, firefighters, police officers, and their allies who waited through long nights to testify at round-the-clock hearings that had been organized by friendly legislators. Democratic state senators who had expected only to cast perfunctory "no" votes as the anti-union legislation advanced toward the governor's desk heard the shouts of "Kill the Bill" from outside and inside the capitol and they bolted, fleeing across the state line in order to deny the Republican majority the quorum it needed to rubber-stamp Walker's agenda. Their exit created the opening for a

4

mass movement to grow and mature, as the rallies and marches spread to communities across the state. Nothing was going as planned for the governor, his party, or their paymasters in the executive suites of distant corporate office towers. But, in truth, nothing was going as planned for the unions or the allies either. This was an uprising, uncharted and uncontrolled, and into the thick of it on the tenth day of the struggle strode the Street Dogs from Boston, Massachusetts.

Along with a pack of legendary rockers, led by Rage Against the Machine guitarist Tom Morello and MC5 guitarist Wayne Kramer, the Street Dogs joined a ragtag band of musicians who had come to sing labor songs for the tens of thousands of workers rallying in the frigid weather outside the capitol. It was an electric moment that saw Wisconsinites, from toddlers to septuagenarians jumping to the most rhythmic version anyone had ever heard of Woody Guthrie's "This Land Is Your Land"—or, perhaps, just jumping in hopes of staying warm. When the official Wisconsin AFL-CIO rally was done, Morello led the crew into the capitol building, where thousands of young teachers, students, and their multigenerational supporters had packed the rotunda and every stairway, hallway, nook, and cranny of the sprawling century-old building that Wisconsinites are taught to revere as the most beautiful statehouse in the nation. The circle of Native American drummers, music students, and their comrades that had formed in the center of the rotunda quieted, as did the chanting of solidarity slogans and the din created when a great building made of marble is filled to capacity. On a first-floor balcony, Leo Gerard, the burly United Steelworkers union president who will never be mistaken for a punk rocker, grabbed a bullhorn and told the crowd, "You have inspired this fat old white guy." Morello, who could be mistaken for a punk rocker, was equally inspired.

Grabbing his own bullhorn, he shouted to the participants in the most sustained mass protest in recent American history:

> Governor Walker . . . didn't count on you. He didn't count on your resolve! This is what they do: in times of economic crisis, they think, "Oh, no, people aren't paying attention, people have all their own worries, so we're going to sneak through this legislation that's going to rob us of decades, maybe a century of social progress." They had the audacity to try to pull that off in Wisconsin. But you people were on guard. We did not pick this fight. He tapped us on the shoulder and said, "Let's fight." And now we're going to knock his legislative teeth out.
>
> They miscalculated. They thought this is going to be the first domino to fall and workers' rights are going to be stripped from them all across the country [Morello continued, as the crowd roared its approval]. They very much miscalculated. This IS going to be the first domino to fall in a new resurgence of labor and student power around this country and around the world. You're setting an unprecedented example—in my lifetime, for this country, for people around the world. Believe it!

They did believe it, and thousands of them accepted his invitation to a free concert in the cavernous basement of the city's convention center. A few hours later, the line of students and young working folks stretched through the hallways of the convention center and out its front door into a night that gave cold comfort to the crowd, as temperatures dipped into the teens, snow fell, and winds whipped off the city's lakes. Inside, however, it was hot. The great claim of those who would dismiss the uprising in Wisconsin has always been that it was "just a bunch of union agitators bused in from around the country." But here, on a February night in the basement of a convention center, were more than five thousand high school and college students from Madison and surrounding communities, most of whom had never been union members, many of whom came from families with no union ties that they knew of. They were hanging on every word spoken about a labor struggle that did not involve them directly, but that would define their futures.

This is where the Street Dogs came in.

The band's lead singer, Mike McColgan, had left a great Irish American punk band, the Dropkick Murphys, in 1998 to become a Boston firefighter, and a proud member of International Association of Fire Fighters Local 718. But McColgan was drawn back to rock and roll during the Bush years. With his new bandmates in the Street Dogs, he broke pattern during that conservative moment and forged an aggressively pro-labor rock band that literally shouted, "Not Without a Purpose, Not Without a Fight!" For years, they had been integrating epic songs like "There Is Power in a Union" and new ones like "Unions and the Law" into sets that sounded as if someone had given Harry Bridges and the San Francisco general strikers of 1934 electric guitars and a stack of Clash CDs. And on this night, this cold and unforgiving winter night in the battleground state of Wisconsin, it all came together as Morello— a musicians' union member who also carries the card of the "one big union," the Industrial Workers of the World— welcomed his fellow stars of the "frostbite and freedom tour."

"How you all doing, Madison Wisconsin?" asked McColgan, as he grabbed the microphone. "It's cold out there and I want to thank all of you for braving the elements, standing your ground and standing up for workers' rights."

As the crowd shouted its approval, he added, "We are from Boston, Massachusetts, and we do not take shit from anybody and we are not going to take shit from Scott Walker or anybody else. So it's cold outside but it's warm in here. We've got a brand new song called 'Up the Union' . . . My hand's in the air and I want you to sing it with me!"

McColgan raised a clenched first, the proud salute of working-class struggles across the ages that just happened to form a shape artists had already recognized as similar enough to an outline of the state of Wisconsin.

Suddenly, all of the passion, all of the energy, all of the sheer unadulterated joy of speaking truth to power in numbers too big to ignore exploded. A thousand fists shot into the air as McColgan sang a new manifesto for a new labor movement:

> Well, it's starting again, a turnaround friend
> A movement of people that want to defend
> Human rights, a fair wage
> A quick return to decent days
>
> Equality is in play
> Workers should organize without haste
> Have the vote in your workplace
> Work with your manager face to face
>
> Look out, it's starting again
> The change, a new labor age

The words had the ring of truth. Not just "that sounds reasonable" or "I guess I agree" truth, but "this is the moment, this is happening now" truth.

It did seem as if something was starting again, something as old as the Wobblies and the Flint sit-down strikers of 1937, something as deep and fundamental as the cry of "solidarity forever" and the promise that "an injury to one is an injury to all," something as meaningful as the moment when the Reverend Martin Luther King linked the civil rights movement and the labor movement on the streets on Memphis in the spring of 1968.

And everybody got it.

McColgan shouted, "Madison, Wisconsin, let's get rowdy! I want to hear you! Sing it with me!" And then he stepped off the stage onto the shoulders of the students who pressed to the front of the hall. Held aloft by the crowd, throwing his fist in the air, he led the chants of "Up the Union! Up the Union!" The response of the students shook the hall.

When he raced on through the song, with its condemnation of the "dedication to corporate greed," its objection that "the pay up top is way too high, while those in the middle barely get by" and its pledge to knock again on the door of economic power with labor might, the closing call—"let's go and start it again"—did not sound idealistic, let alone unrealistic. It sounded right and good and necessary. And when the guitars and the drums went silent and McColgan shouted "Do it!" the fists were still held high and teenagers and college students shouted back, "Yes! Do it!"

This was more than just interesting or "notable" or "newsworthy." This was remarkable, and inspiring. Commentators on these times do not turn with comfort or frequency to such words. Tom Paine is long gone. And so are Horace Greeley, Ida B. Wells and I. F. Stone. The credo of what passes for journalism these days respects cynicism rather than optimism; editors and reporters have for the most part become guardians against any leap of faith. Don't hesitate to describe the most horrific tragedy in the most painful detail, the counsel of the craft goes.

But be careful when it comes to suggesting that change is in the air, that the folks who have been on the losing end of a long class war might finally choose to fight back or, heaven forbid, that the next generation might not be so easily duped as those that came before.

The fear of hope, so palpable in so many pundits and pontificators, is not just a bow to the status quo, not just due deference to the powerful. Even among the most progressive observers, there is a disinclination to employ the language of possibility, for fear of stirring false faith—and, just as important, for fear of being identified as one who dares to reject diminished expectations and believe that what is to come might actually be better than what was. After all, these have not been progressive times; even when the people have chosen leaders who promise "change we can believe in," they have been repaid with "compromise we cannot understand or justify."

But on this winter night in the middle of America, the only reasonable response is to believe.

For as long as I can remember, sincere and savvy labor activists and their lefty allies have wrestled with the question of how to reach out to "the youth." I'm not talking about the romantics longing to recreate some experience they had at Berkeley in 1966, or outside the Pentagon in 1967, or at Columbia in 1968, or even at Woodstock in 1969. I'm talking about veteran organizers who put real energy into making connections across generational lines, with an eye toward engaging young people in struggles of consequence for themselves in a country characterized by child poverty, youth unemployment, skyrocketing tuition costs, and still, as George McGovern observed a half century ago, by "old men dreaming up wars for young men to die in." The labor movement has cracked the code a few times in recent decades. Many of the smartest and most committed radicals of the 1960s and 1970s made lifetime commitments to organize, maintain, and lead unions. They knew that organized labor would have a future only if young people continued to be drawn to the faith that life was more than a get-rich-quick scheme and the principle that an injury to one really is an injury to all. The best and the brightest—Baldemar Velasquez, David Newby, Bruce Colburn, Rose Ann DeMoro, and the others who initiated movement-conscious projects like the farm labor organizing and "Justice for Janitors" campaigning of the 1980s, the groundbreaking anti-sweatshop work of the Student Labor Action Coalition during the 1990s, and the mass protests against the corporate-friendly globalization regime of the World Trade Organization that shook Seattle in 1999—all invited a next generation of activists into the struggle. Unfortunately, "struggle" was precisely the right word; making the connection, and keeping it alive, were never easy.

But what I saw in Madison, on that February night and across the days and nights of February and March and April, what I see even now, months later, as the uprising in Wisconsin continues and fresh variations play out in the Occupy Wall Street movement, is different. The connection was made, and not just at one show or for one night. The high school and college students showed up, again and again and again, for rallies, marches, and vigils. They learned the intricacies of pieces of legislation and political processes. And they did so on their own terms: with the energy, the passion, the steadiness of vision and purpose that reminds older activists that idealism at its best comes with an edge. It was that edge that flashed when Mike McColgan shouted, "Do it!" Something real was happening, something palpable.

I could not help recalling on that rare and remarkable night the response of Claude Lévi-Strauss to requests that he identify the "golden age" of human civilization. Surely, as the father of modern anthropology, the great student of the human experience, the scholar was presumed to know when the best of times had been, or perhaps when, under the right circumstances, they might come to pass. Lévi-Strauss always rejected these questions as absurd on their face, and absurdly disempowering in their implications.

In *Tristes Tropiques*, Lévi-Strauss explained that "if men have always been concerned with only one task—how to create a society fit to live in—the forces which inspired our distant ancestors are also present in us. Nothing is settled; everything can still be altered. What was done but turned out wrong, can be done again. The Golden Age, which blind superstition had placed behind [or ahead of] us, is in us." Those are not blandly optimistic words. They are demanding. They suggest that we have fewer excuses than we thought, that this is the place, that now is the time, and that there is truth in the Gandhian maxim that we are the people we've been waiting for. Since the middle of February 2011, I have been asked hundreds of times, perhaps thousands, "What's happening in Wisconsin?" It's never an inquiry about specific events or a request for a news report. What people are really seeking is an explanation. Why? How? At a point when it seemed the long project of corporate empowerment was finally succeeding in creating a "new normal" where the parameters of the American experiment had been narrowed to allow for a range of debate that began on the right and moved toward the abyss, what was it that made a whole state rise up in open revolt against a governor who pushed too far and a lie that says organized labor, social-justice movements, and democracy itself are relics to be tossed aside in a headlong rush to redistribute the wealth of nations upward?

A lot of organizing went into what worked in Wisconsin. Some of that organizing began a century ago, with the work of Robert M. La Follette's progressives and Milwaukee's muscular Socialist Party. Some of it began in the months before Scott Walker took office, when it was already evident to teachers' unions and the representatives of public employees that a fight was brewing.

But organizing, no matter how epic in scope, no matter how honorable in purpose, no matter how meticulous in planning, is necessarily prologue. At some point, if there is to be a new labor age, or for that matter a golden age, it must begin. This is the story of that beginning.

CHAPTER 2

First Amendment Remedies

A Reclaiming of the
Constitution's Rules for Radicals

Justice is the end of government. It is the end of civil society. It ever has been and ever will be pursued until it be obtained, or until liberty be lost in the pursuit.
—Publius (James Madison), "Federalist No. 51," 1788

We have long rested comfortably in this country upon the assumption that because our form of government was democratic, it was therefore automatically producing democratic results. Now, there is nothing mysteriously potent about the forms and names of democratic institutions that should make them self-operative. Tyranny and oppression are just as possible under democratic forms as under any other. We are slow to realize that democracy is a life; and involves continual struggle. It is only as those of every generation who love democracy resist with all their might the encroachments of its enemies that the ideals of representative government can even be nearly approximated.
—Robert M. La Follette, November 11, 1911

This is a King moment. Dr. King knew that when the machinery of government is corrupted, when our political leaders fail us, we must march, we must rally, we must demonstrate. We have a right to assemble and my how you have assembled!

—Rev. Jesse Jackson, Madison, Wisconsin, February 18, 2011

JAMES MADISON would have approved.

This, for reasons of history and the current state of the American crisis that Madison's troublesome comrade Tom Paine first described in 1777, is the place to begin any consideration of why Wisconsin matters.

That the first great expressions of the revolt against right-wing authoritarianism of the moment were seen on the streets of the only American capital city named for the essential author of the Constitution is a consideration. But the pitch-perfect utilization of the rights Madison enumerated in the first amendment to the Constitution by those who revolted, and the example they set for others who would revolt outside capitols in Lansing and Columbus, on Freedom Plaza in Washington and at Zuccotti Park in Lower Manhattan, this, this above all, is what would have delighted the founder who wrestled most ardently with questions about the role the people would play in defending the American experiment against all enemies foreign and domestic.

★ ★ ★

MR. MADISON WAS a fretful revolutionary, a cautious radical who well understood the honest stance of the patriot in the immediate aftermath of the creation of these United States to be that of the utopian pessimist. He recognized that the intrigues in which he and his rebellious contemporaries were engaged had the potential to inspire the world to throw off the chains of brutish superstition and crude complacency. But he was certain that new forms of superstition and complacency would be turned against not just the American experiment but the cause of liberty itself.

Romantic fools and their historian apologists often perceive the American founding as a black-and-white image of prim plantation owners in powdered wigs, very proper, very responsible, very English in all but name. The truth of the founding has always been more complex and multihued. The American Revolution, guided as it was by enlightenment principles, held out the promise of a new course, and in those days of innocent faith in progress, a new course might still be imagined as ending at the destination of the perfect. But only the most naive of the rebels considered their course to have been divinely charted, or assuredly constant. The realists in the revolutionary circle recognized the threat posed by the pull of the past, by the conservative impulse that would seek not perfection but a return to the colonial furrow, with its crudely dictated class lines, its authoritarianism, and above all its stingy measure of hope for an evolution of the human condition. Power, both economic and political, always asserts itself for the purpose of retaining its privileges and restoring the presumed birthrights of the elite that have been lost to reform or revolution. This Madison knew all too well as the great tension that would forever afflict any people who sought to break the grip of royalism, be it political or economic. He feared nothing so much as factions controlled by the wealthy and organized for the purpose of dictating the return to an old order; foretelling the rise of contemporary movements, such as an ironically misnamed "Tea Party" project that demands a return to the colonial calculus of an undertaxed elite riding "booted and spurred" atop the great mass of citizens. Today's national discourse, with its fantastical debates about cutting services for the great mass of citizens in order to fund the good life of the one percent at the top, was one that the essential founder sought to guard against during the unsettled moment when Americans decided whether theirs was to be a United States.

The utopian-pessimist tension came to a head after Madison had secured approval at the 1787 convention in Philadelphia for a constitution constructed at every turn with an eye toward checking and balancing the consolidation of power in the hands of an individual or faction that was inclined toward the self-service, the corruption, and the perpetuation of authority that Madison knew to be "kingly oppressions."

Madison hoped the document approved in Philadelphia, with all of its delicate balances and compromises, would be a sufficient beginning for the republic. But the veterans of the Revolution, warier even than Madison not just of foreign kings but of domestic elites, were unsatisfied. They demanded a bill of rights in return for approval of a model of government that vested power in executive and legislative branches that, while formally representative, could become every bit as distant and dastardly as the crown. Madison recognized that they were right and, in the spirit of those times of national invention, he put that recognition to the test: campaigning to represent his Virginia constituency in the first Congress on a platform that began and ended with a pledge to properly amend the Constitution. "If all power is subject to abuse ... then it is possible the abuse of the powers of the General Government may be guarded against in a more secure manner than is now done," he informed his colleagues in the U.S. House, counseling that the amendments must outline rights with the purpose of assuring "that the people have an indubitable, unalienable, and indefeasible right to reform or change their Government, whenever it be found adverse or inadequate to the purposes of its institution."

When Wisconsinites exercised their indubitable, unalienable, and indefeasible rights, they were greeted by the Tories of this age with the same sort of abuse that was directed at the Revolutionaries of 1776, and at the champions of the Bill of Rights in 1789. The only difference is that the Tories of today claim—comically, perhaps, but constantly—to be the constitutional Knights Templar, the contemporary defenders of a one true faith expressed in a seemingly incoherent patois of political paranoia, states-rights nostalgia, and anti-democratic delusion that sounds like nothing so much as the secret-handshake intrigues and the dark mumblings of a John Birch Society meeting in Bakersfield, circa 1962.

The false prophets of original intent have so warped the discussion of all things constitutional that a newcomer to the American story, stumbling upon a Glenn Beck podcast or a "Herman Cain for President" rally might imagine that the document penned by militant anti-imperialists who had only recently concluded a violent revolution against their colonial overlords was a conservative outline for controlling rather than liberating the masses.

It is certainly true that nothing so horrifies today's false constitutionalists as the actual exercise of civil liberties.

But it is also true that nothing so frightened the most serious of the founders as the notion that their revolution might eventually be perverted by "the unwise and unworthy passions" of those who would make useless the sacrifices of Thomas Jefferson's "generation of 1776." The whole point of the endeavor was to unsettle and ultimately disempower the puffed and powdered elites who imagined themselves forever superior to the "equal daughters, equal sons" in whom Walt Whitman found "the genius of the United States." Whitman urged his Jeffersonian masses to "resist much, obey little," and this was the intent of those who engaged in what the poet of democracy hailed as "the peerless, passionate good cause." Jefferson, the author of the Declaration of Independence and counselor to Madison in the drafting of the Constitution and Bill of Rights said as much in his last reflection on the revolutionary impulse:

> May [July 4] be to the world, what I believe it will be—to some parts sooner, to others later, but finally to all—the signal of arousing men to burst the chains under which monkish ignorance and superstition had persuaded them to bind themselves, and to assume the blessings and security of self-government. That form (of government) which we have substituted, restores the free right to the unbounded exercise of reason and freedom of opinion. All eyes are opened, or opening, to the rights of man. The general spread of the light of science has already laid open to every view the palpable truth, that the mass of mankind has not been born with saddles on their backs, nor a favored few booted and spurred, ready to ride them legitimately, by the grace of God.

★ ★ ★

THE WINTER SOLDIERS of Wisconsin, circa 2011, burst the chains of contemporary Toryism and resumed the blessings of security and self-government that belonged to them—not to the British East India Company or Koch Industries, not to colonial governors serving distant kings or contemporary governors serving distant corporations.

The fight in Wisconsin, and in the states that joined the battle for labor rights and small "d" democracy as it spread across the country in the late winter and early spring of 2011, revealed who the true constitutionalists were. And in so doing it changed the discussion on the ground in communities across the country, even if the politicians and pundits who would set themselves up as the arbiters of the Constitution continued to spin their Tory fantasies. The assembling of the people to petition for the redress of grievances was not a new phenomenon. As he prepared to speak to more than fifty thousand Wisconsinites on the steps of the capitol one week into the struggle, Rev. Jesse Jackson mused, "This is a King moment. Dr. King knew that when the machinery of government is corrupted, when our political leaders fail us, we must march, we must rally, we must demonstrate. We have a right to assemble and my how you have assembled!"

It was a Rev. Dr. Martin Luther King Jr. moment.

But it was, as well, a James Madison moment. A Thomas Jefferson moment. A Tom Paine moment. An American moment.

This was lost on the political grifters who have tried to claim a secular Constitution that outlines the framework for a civil society as an instrument of religious and corporate grasping.

For too long, in a moment characterized by managed media and misguided discourse, the grifters dominated the discourse. They even tried to shout down the uprising in Wisconsin.

Anyone who was ever caught in an airport lounge where a television set was locked on the Fox News channel knew where things were headed even before the citizens of Wisconsin began to assemble.

Yes, of course, the organizer of Washington's Constitutional Conservative Caucus, Minnesota congresswoman Michele Bachmann, would dismiss the Wisconsin protests as "beyond conscionable" and suggest that teachers who protested might be due the same treatment that Ronald Reagan meted out to air traffic controllers when they struck in 1981: firing. (Bachmann lives in a nether world where irony is unknown, so it is only for the amusement of others that it will be noted that King George III's minions fired no less a patriot than Tom Paine for trying to organize an eighteenth-century version of a public employees' union.)

Yes, of course, conservative provocateur Ann Coulter would ridicule the handmade signs that filled the squares of small towns and cities across Wisconsin because they referenced the rights of working people (as opposed, presumably, to tax-evading CEOs)—just as she would dismiss citizens who dared challenge a a long train of abuses and usurpations designed to reduce them under absolute despotism as "demonic."

Yes, of course, talk radio's Rush Limbaugh would condemn the marches and rallies by Wisconsin workers, farmers, teachers, and students as "thuggery," "mob-ocracy" and "an anti-democratic movement." Dismissing the protesters as "union thugs," Limbaugh ridiculed "the same old traditional argument; the rights of working people are being trampled on," as if the fact that the rights of working people were being trampled on, and had been trampled on for a long time, was rendered irrelevant by the mere use of the term "union thugs."

But conservative "constitutionalists" have always read the founding document with convenient eyes that are as blind to the intents and ideals of the founders as were those of their Tory ancestors. They do fear the mob, the mass, the people, and, above all, the prospect that democracy might be defined as something more than the exercise in futility that so many elections have become in an era of unlimited corporate cash and empty partisanship.

But the conservative "constitutionalists," who for so long had controlled the conversation, were about to find themselves in a debate with the true patriots of the contemporary American turning. And the patriots had history on their side.

★ ★ ★

THE REVOLT that swept Wisconsin during those frigid weeks of February and March 2011—drawing hundreds of thousands of workers, farmers, students, and retirees into the streets and upsetting the political order to such an extent that the agenda of the most powerful corporate titans and their elected handmaidens was delayed and diminished—had its truest roots in the long hot constitutional summer of 1787 and the even longer striving to form a republic where citizens would have the authority to check and balance the factions that might turn the governing process into a tool of the economic elites.

America is still occupied with the great struggle between the Madisonian faithful, operating on the founding premise that the people are the only certain defenders of the republic, and those who would consolidate power for political and financial gain. The fabulists who imagine a progress that absolves citizens of their watchman duties are always proven wrong. The late-in-life counsel of Madison's mentor and friend, Jefferson, remains the watchword: "Independence can be trusted nowhere but with the people in mass."

That the appearance in the late winter of 2011 of the people in mass so unsettled the powerful—not just Governor Walker and his legislative allies but the whole of the conservative echo chamber, which remains obsessed with the "threat" posed by popular agitation—ought not come as any surprise. In their correspondence during the summer of 1787, when Jefferson advised from Paris as Madison crafted the Constitution at the convention in Philadelphia, the pair of future presidents ruminated at great length regarding the certainty that power would corrupt. And on the certain necessity of filling the town square, surrounding the capital, and causing the corrupt and corrosive occupants of stations of public trust to quake in the face of what would two centuries later come to be known as "people power." "*Malo periculosam libertatem quam quietum servitutium* [I prefer the tumult of liberty to the quiet of servitude]. Even this evil is productive of good. It prevents the degeneracy of government, and nourishes a general attention to the public affairs," Jefferson argued in a letter from Paris, written around the same time that he would observe, "The spirit of resistance to government is so valuable on certain occasions, that I wish it to be always kept alive. It will often be exercised when wrong, but better so than not to be exercised at all. I like a little rebellion now and then. It is like a storm in the atmosphere."

It is not possible to appreciate the full significance or the potential of what happened in Madison, Milwaukee, Ashland and Appleton, Wausau and Wauwatosa at the opening of the second decade of the twenty-first century without recalling that the wisest of the founders had three centuries earlier imagined just such moments. And that they put in place not only electoral models, which they outlined only vaguely, but specific tools for challenging the abuses and excesses of an "elected despotism."

The wisest of the founders, those who arrived at the revolutionary moment steeped already in the enlightenment teachings of their time, recognized that the fact of a candidate's election did not prevent him from assuming the trappings of monarchy. Every executive, argued the man who would serve two terms as the nation's fourth president, should be viewed skeptically by the citizen. "The limitation of the period of his service was not a sufficient power," Madison warned. "He might pervert his administration into a scheme of peculation or oppression. He might betray his trust."

And he might not act on his own.

The despotism Madison feared was not merely that of an American king. He recognized that it could take the form of "factions": political cabals held together by the joint ambition and greed of their leaders. Factions, he worried, would come to control government so completely that they could game not just executive decisions and the legislative process but judicial deliberations and the electoral process itself.

So it was that Madison arrived at Philadelphia in 1787 with a vision of representative government that would make elected leaders "the agents and trustees for the people" rather than the masters they had been in the empire against which the framers had so recently revolted. Constraints on leaders, both structural and political, were necessary because, as Madison observed, "Since the general civilization of mankind, I believe there are more instances of the abridgment of the freedom of the people by silent encroachments of those in power, than by violent and sudden usurpations." It was in response to this concern that the basic document approved in Philadelphia at the close of that long summer of 1787 outlined protections against such executive overreach: a system of checks and balances, divided authority, and tools for the impeachment and swift removal of errant officials. But with his comrade Jefferson, Madison soon came to understand that the outline was insufficient to win the approval of Americans who were concerned with "securing to themselves and posterity the liberties they had gained by an arduous conflict." What constitutional historian Pauline Maier describes as "the dialogue between power and liberty" had been translated from the international stage, where an empire faced the revolt of colonists, to the domestic stage, where the former colonists demanded a clear definition of their authority to guard against "kingly oppressions."

Madison's recognition of the necessity of attaching a bill of rights to the document he had crafted so carefully at Philadelphia did not evolve through reading or scholarly discourse. It came on the campaign trail, in a remarkable election race for a seat in the U.S. House of Representatives. It had been presumed that Madison would become a senator in the first Congress. But his archenemy, Patrick Henry, used his authority as governor and his alliances in the Virginia legislature to deny Madison a seat in the upper chamber. Henry then arranged the gerrymandering of Virginia's U.S. House districts so that Madison would be forced to run against another future president, James Monroe, for the seat representing his home at Montpelier. Madison prevailed over the popular Monroe by promising to secure congressional approval for a bill of rights. This he did, joining the Congress as a man on a mission.

"I conclude," Madison told the House in an address proposing the Bill of Rights, "that it will be proper in itself, and highly politic, for the tranquillity of the public mind, and the stability of the Government, that we should offer something, in the form I have proposed, to be incorporated in the system of Government, as a declaration of the rights of the people."

Most of the protections outlined by Madison were defensive: "effectual provision against encroachments on particular rights." There were safeguards against unreasonable search and seizure, excessive bail, self-incrimination, and double jeopardy; there were restrictions against the quartering of troops in private homes and the application of those cruel and unusual punishments that most Americans (with the unsettling exceptions of recent presidents and attorneys general) understand as torture.

But Madison also spoke of the need to "specify positive rights, which may seem to result from the nature of the compact."

Chief among these were the guarantees that Americans could challenge an elected despotism when it arose, rather than merely waiting until the next election. These were the rights outlined by Madison when he identified a first amendment to the Constitution that promised:

> The people shall not be deprived or abridged of their right to speak, to write, or to publish their sentiments; and the freedom of the press, as one of the great bulwarks of liberty, shall be inviolable.

> The people shall not be restrained from peaceably assembling and consulting for their common good; nor from applying to the Legislature by petitions, or remonstrances, for redress of their grievances.

These bulwarks of liberty were not confirmed merely as tools for tempering the excesses of a federal government but also for the states. Indeed, Madison suggested to the first Congress, on that definitional day in 1789, that it was wise and necessary to impose "a doubt security" against abuses of liberty by state governments. "I think there is more danger of those powers being abused by the state governments than by the government of the United States," he explained. "The same may be said of other powers which they possess, if not controlled by the general principle, that laws are unconstitutional which infringe the rights of the community."

Madison's arguments prevailed, winning the approval of the House and Senate as summer turned to fall, and forwarding the amendments that would form a bill of rights to the states for the deliberations that would finally and fully realize the promise of the American Revolution.

★ ★ ★

WITH THE MATURING of the American experiment in the first decades of the nineteenth century, the founding circle began to die off. As the circle shrank, Jefferson feared the radical ideals of the Revolution and the vision that informed its Constitution were dying, as well. Six years before his own death, on the fiftieth anniversary of the Continental Congress's approval of the Declaration of Independence he had penned, Jefferson wrote to a friend:

> I regret that I am now to die in the belief, that the useless sacrifice of themselves by the generation of 1776, to acquire self-government and happiness to their country, is to be thrown away by the unwise and unworthy passions of their sons, and that my only consolation is to be, that I live not to weep over it. If they would but dispassionately weigh the blessings they will throw away, against an abstract principle more likely to be effected by union than by scission, they would pause before they would perpetrate this act of suicide on themselves, and of treason against the hopes of the world.

After Jefferson and Adams were buried, and then Monroe, as well, Madison came to recognize himself as a lonely defender of the "spirit of '76" that he and Jefferson had understood in

very nearly mystical terms. The last surviving signer of the Declaration of Independence, Charles Carroll of Maryland, died in
1832. The last signer of the Articles of Confederation, William
Ellery of Rhode Island, had been buried a dozen years earlier.
William Few of Georgia, the final remaining signer of the Constitution aside from Madison, breathed his last in 1828.

So it was that Madison lived his final years as the sole remaining Founding Father, an honor that the former president
wore as a heavy burden. Obsessed with threats he believed were
posed to liberty by long wars and foreign entanglements, by
the expansion of executive powers, by the mingling of religion
and politics (one of his last essays framed an argument against
the appointment of chaplains for the Congress and the military), Madison was said by biographer Drew McCoy to have
been at times "literally sick with anxiety, he began to despair
of his ability to make himself understood by his fellow citizens."
At age seventy-eight, he agreed to serve as a delegate to the
convention charged with revising Virginia's state constitution.
But he despaired at the refusal of powerful plantation owners
to expand the franchise to those who did not own land, and to
apportion representation based on population. Fearing that the
landed aristocracy was shutting down avenues for checking and
balancing the authority of a state government that a narrow
elite defined and controlled, Madison warned the convention
that "the essence of Government is power; and power, lodged
as it must be in human hands, will ever be liable to abuse."

This determination to assert and reassert the principle that
the people could and should be the true guardians of liberty
and their rights would earn Madison high praise from historian Garry Wills, who affirmed that "as a framer and defender
of the Constitution he had no peer." But as the mortal coil
loosened, Madison became ever more fretful that the people

would fail to recognize their power and their responsibility. Madison's death, in the summer of 1836 at age eighty-five, came sixty years after the Declaration of Independence was drafted, forty-nine years after the Constitution was drafted, and forty-seven years after he determined that he must lead the fight to attach to the latter document a bill of rights. The nation was on the verge of its first great financial panic, as speculators unleashed waves of inflation and deflation and unemployment reached record levels. Steam locomotives were carrying passengers and goods on an evolving system of railroads. Samuel Morse was developing the telegraph. A young veteran of the Black Hawk War, Abraham Lincoln, was seeking his second term as an Illinois state legislator. A mere twenty-four years later, Lincoln would be elected to the presidency and a civil war, which Madison's last writings anticipated, would begin.

In a moment of such turmoil and transition, Madison's death was well noted but did not inspire the renewal of the founding faith that the fourth president and his friend Jefferson had hoped might follow upon the last passing of their founding generation. Except, intriguingly, in a western outpost where a former federal judge was laying out the city he hoped would become the capital of the Wisconsin Territory. In the summer of 1836, James Duane Doty named the city that existed primarily in his imagination "Madison." But he did not stop there; before the year was done, he and a civil engineer named James Slaughter had laid out the streets of Madison, naming them for the thirty-nine signers of the Constitution.

★ ★ ★

ONE HUNDRED and seventy five years later, near the corner of two of those streets—Pinckney (named for a young South Carolina firebrand, Charles Pinckney, who aligned with Jefferson and Madison to defend the still-fresh Constitution from the Alien and Sedition Act abuse of then-president John Adams) and Washington (named for the commander of the Continental Army who refused encouragement that he accept the title of king after the Revolutionary War was done, and who willingly accepting the constraints on the presidency imposed by the Constitution)—I encountered David Vines.

A University of Wisconsin student who joined the first of the mass protests against Governor Walker's attempts to strip public employee unions of their collective bargaining rights, to do away with muscular trade unions, and to constrain our politics so that only Walker's allies would be heard at election time, Vines explained to me how he recognized that Wisconsin was being threatened with precisely the sort of elected despotism against which the best of the founders warned.

He was not the only protester to reach that conclusion.

Over the weeks and months to come, the thousands, then tens of thousands, then hundreds of thousands of Wisconsinites who joined the struggle to avert Walker's agenda would recognize a steady pattern of assaults on basic liberties and the very underpinnings of self-governance.

Walker claimed that budget deficits necessitated his actions, but it soon became clear that Wisconsin was suffering from a different kind of deficit crisis. It was not the budget crisis about which so many pundits and politicians prattled on and on; that was a minor challenge that could have been addressed with fair taxation and smart priorities. The deficit that was taxing Wisconsin was far more severe.

Wisconsin's crisis, it became clear, resulted from a democracy deficit. And citizens recognized that if they did not address it immediately and effectively, the state that a century earlier had been hailed as America's "laboratory of democracy" would instead see a degeneration of politics and policy making that would come to serve as a model of worst practices for the nation.

The circumstance was dire, as any detailing of developments beginning in February of 2011 would well confirm to even the most casual small "d" democrat:

1. Governor Walker and his allies proposed to deny basic labor rights to state, county, and municipal employees and teachers, as part of a grand plan not merely to silence voices in the workplace but to undermine the ability of working people to make their collective voices heard in political and policy-making debates.

2. Confronted by some of the largest peaceful protests in recent American history, Wisconsin's governor threatened to call out the National Guard, openly discussed employing agent provocateurs to stir "false-flag" violence, and connived to end the historic practice of keeping the state capitol open to the people.

3. Republican leaders of the two houses of the state legislature disregarded the state's open meetings law, failed to hold public hearings on major pieces of legislation, closed votes before assembly members could participate, and threatened to arrest, fine, and deny voting privileges to dissenting legislators.

4. Proposals were advanced to deny local elected school boards the authority to make basic decisions about charter schools and education policy and to prevent elected town boards from setting budget standards.

5. Legislative allies of the governor moved to amend the state constitution to end the election of the secretary of state, the state treasurer and justices of the state supreme court.

6. The chairman of the powerful Joint Finance Committee proposed to amend the eighty-five-year-old provision in the state constitution that outlined provisions for the recall and removal of elected officials. The proposed amendment, sought as a campaign to recall Governor Walker ramped up in the fall of 2011, was designed to make it dramatically harder for citizens to use the recall as an accountability tool.

7. The closest state supreme court election in modern Wisconsin history was marred by irregularities so severe that a veteran member of Congress, Representative Tammy Baldwin, D-Madison, asked the U.S. Department of Justice to intervene.

8. The most restrictive "voter ID" law in the nation was enacted over the objections of the League of Women Voters, Common Cause, and other civic groups in Wisconsin and across the country, inspiring complaints that political players were writing laws with the purpose of suppressing voter participation.

9. The redistricting process was restructured to dismiss the concerns and needs of Wisconsin communities while drawing maps that divided cities, denied minority representation, and virtually eliminated competitive state senate districts. The new maps drew outspoken opponents of the governor's actions, such as fiery young state representative Cory Mason, out of the districts that elected them, virtually assuring that the loudest and most effective dissenters against Walker's agenda would not be returned to the next legislature.

10. Recall elections for nine state senate seats, held in July and August of 2011, saw more than $43 million in spending, much of it by unaccountable out-of-state groups, in an orgy of negative campaigning that led one of the senior Republi-

cans in the state legislature to suggest that candidates and citizens were being left on the political wayside, as bystanders to their own elections. "For the first time in the history of Wisconsin politics—and you can print this—candidates are now almost irrelevant to campaigns," said Senate President Mike Ellis. "They have hijacked these elections—both sides. And the candidates have nothing to do with it."

Only in the most crudely drawn Orwellian fantasy could this bill of particulars be described along the lines that champions of Scott Walker's heresy attempted: as a new, "streamlined" model of liberty. The models in play were those of the American Legislative Exchange Council (ALEC), a corporation-funded "bill mill," which drew up anti-consumer, anti-union and, above all, anti-democracy legislation for pliant conservative legislators in Wisconsin, Ohio, Michigan, and states across the country to introduce and enact.

There was nothing of liberty to be found in the ALEC agenda. Nor was there anything new about it. This was the old Toryism of King George's followers, repackaged by the Brothers Koch and the politicians they have hired to make an America fit for billionaires and Birchers.

The financiers of ALEC and a Tea Party movement that has as its purpose the figurative restoration of the British East India Company fortunes that were so affronted at Boston Harbor have adopted the language of reform and revolution. But they are not in the business of giving power to the people. And they are certainly not intent upon breaking the grip of empire, be it kingly or corporate, along the lines intended by the attendees of the Tea Party of 1773. Indeed, if there are any self-evident truths in the projects of today's Tories, they are exposed in their fear of popular democracy, open government, and free elections.

The grievances imposed upon Wisconsin in 2011 by Scott Walker and his cronies represented way stations on a road map to ruin, not just for one state but for an American experiment that has always been more fragile than those Paine derided as sunshine patriots would have us imagine.

The stations would not all be reached immediately. But as they were encountered, the scope of the threat became clear: this was the dismantling and diminishment of democracy in one state and the model for a similar dismantling and diminishment in every state and, ultimately, in Washington. It was well recognized, as such, by Wisconsinites, then by their allies in Ohio and other states, and eventually the young people who would gather on Wall Street in the fall of 2011 for the stated purpose of "protecting our democracy."

The starting point in Wisconsin came where despots invariably begin: with an assault on the right of the disconnected mass of citizens to assemble themselves into the powerful political force that is a strong trade union. The signs at the capitol read LABOR RIGHTS ARE HUMAN RIGHTS in recognition of the greatest rule for radicals: that the only way to counter organized money, and the oligarchy it seeks to create, is with organized people. Walker's attack on Wisconsin's public employee and public education unions was the opening salvo in an assault on democracy that—unless halted—would continue until the elected despots had succeeded in gaming the electoral system so they might never face a meaningful challenge.

David Vines understood, instinctively and immediately, what was at stake.

And he knew what to do.

This political science student, who on the night I met him would join thousands of other Wisconsinites who were sleeping in the capitol to make sure the legislature did not approve

Walker's assault on labor rights without a fight, got a particular subtlety of the Constitution that the political leaders who swear oaths to defend the document's principles frequently miss.

It was the Madisonian point, the Jeffersonian point.

The Constitution is not just a framework for government with a few defensive statements about basic rights attached. It is a charge to preserve the republic against enemies foreign and domestic, which outlines in the First Amendment the strategies and tactics—the rules for radicals, if you will—to be employed in such endeavors.

When I asked Vines why he had put aside his studies to march, rally, and even sleep in the capitol, he replied, "This is what the founders intended."

The response was the one James Madison and Thomas Jefferson were waiting for, hoping for, when they fell to fretting about the liability of power to abuse and "the useless sacrifice of themselves by the generation of 1776."

As a defender of the radical reading of the Constitution in essays and books written over the better part of two decades, it was the response I had always believed could still be mustered, even in an America where so much punditry, so much political positioning, and so much of the money power steers our experiment further and further from its revolutionary moorings.

All the forces of punditry, politics, and the money power were, indeed, conspiring to thwart a popular response to Walker's assault on democracy itself.

But the reality of what was happening was not lost on David Vines, or the hundreds of thousands of Wisconsinites who would eventually join him in protesting, petitioning, and campaigning against the "kingly oppressions" of Scott Walker's regime.

This time, the spin that the political and economic elites had developed to scare citizens into sacrificing not just their largesse but their rights was rejected.

When Democratic members of the Wisconsin state senate walked out of the capitol on the night I met Vines, denying the Republican majority the quorum necessary to pass the legislation on the rapid schedule established by the governor, they were attacked by Walker and his cronies. The governor called the boycott a "stunt" and claimed the Democrats were disrespecting democracy.

After all, Walker and his backers noted, the governor and the Republican majorities in the state assembly and senate were freshly arrived from the electoral victories that so many Republicans enjoyed in 2010.

The fact of their success at the polls the previous November was not open to debate.

But Jefferson warned against placing too much faith in elections, and too little in an active citizenry. "If once [the people] become inattentive to the public affairs, you and I, and Congress and Assemblies, Judges and Governors, shall all become wolves," the future president counseled in the year of the federal Constitution's framing.

Those who embraced the Jeffersonian and Madisonian faith in 1787 and across the decades and centuries that followed always recognized this as the essential understanding, and requirement, of citizenship.

★ ★ ★

WISCONSIN'S GREATEST governor, Robert M. La Follette, expressed this faith when he warned in the era of the robber barons that "we have long rested comfortably in this country upon the assumption that because our form of government was democratic, it was therefore automatically producing democratic results. Now, there is nothing mysteriously potent about the forms and names of democratic institutions that should make them self-operative. Tyranny and oppression are just as possible under democratic forms as under any other. We are slow to realize that democracy is a life; and involves continual struggle. It is only as those of every generation who love democracy resist with all their might the encroachments of its enemies that the ideals of representative government can even be nearly approximated."

La Follette's point, lost on Scott Walker and so many of his apologists but well understood by the crowds that filled the capitol and the streets around it to protest an assault on liberty in the winter of 2011, was that democracy does not end on election day. That's when it begins. Citizens do not elect officials to rule them from one election to the next. Citizens elect officials to represent them, to respond to the popular will as it evolves. And when those officials err against that will, they must legitimately and justifiably suffer the consequence that Jefferson alluded to when he hailed the power of the people to serve as "a censor before which the most exalted tremble for their future."

Conservative zealots may imagine that violence is the only effective counterbalance to what they perceive as an "elected despotism." So it was that Nevada U.S. Senate candidate Sharon Angle famously suggested as her 2010 campaign advanced, "You know, our Founding Fathers, they put that Second Amendment in there for a good reason and that was for the people to protect themselves against a tyrannical government. And in fact Thomas Jefferson said it's good for a country to have a revolution every twenty years. I hope that's not where we're going, but, you know, if this Congress keeps going the way it is, people are really looking toward those Second Amendment remedies and saying my goodness, what can we do to turn this country around?"

But the Wisconsinites who took to the streets to protest an assault on labor rights arrived with a deeper understanding of the Constitution's full promise, rather than a narrow reading of the document as the property of a single ideology.

There are already many assessments of what was done right and what was done wrong in Wisconsin, of which strategies worked and which did not, of genius moves and monumental missteps. But the truest accomplishment of the protests in Madison and cities across Wisconsin was that they renewed an understanding of citizens not merely as voters in elections but as active censors of an elected despotism that can never be allowed to go unchallenged.

The sign David Vines carried as he marched on that Thursday in February 2011, demanded FIRST AMENDMENT REMEDIES! What did he mean? Read the First Amendment: "Congress shall make no law respecting an establishment of religion, or prohibiting the free exercise thereof; or abridging the freedom of speech, or of the press; or the right of the people peaceably to assemble, and to petition the Government for a redress of grievances."

The founders, fresh from a revolution against an imperial monarch and his crown corporations, did not outline a right of the people peaceably to assemble so that folks could get together to attend a baseball game, or even to see the Green Bay Packers win a Super Bowl.

The founders did not guarantee a right to petition the government for a redress of grievances so that Americans could gripe about the cold winter.

The purpose of the First Amendment, the essential amendment for those who believe in a real and robust democracy experiment, was to detail the rights of citizens to object when wrongheaded and dangerous policies are proposed by their elected officials.

This is what happened in Wisconsin in those remarkable weeks after Governor Walker announced that he would use a budget repair bill to dismantle labor rights.

Fourteen Democratic state senators, acting not as rulers but as the elected representatives of the people, looked out the windows of the state capitol and saw their constituents assembling peaceably to petition for the redress of grievances. "Tens of thousands of Wisconsinites were demanding to be heard," explained state senator Mark Miller, the Democratic minority leader in the chamber. "We heard them."

The senators made the choice to withdraw their consent from the rush to judgment by the Republican leadership of the legislature. They exited the capitol and left the state, denying Republican leaders the quorum they needed to enact Walker's anti-labor agenda. That provided the time that was needed for a series of protests to evolve into a movement that would eventually remove from office Republican senators who did not heed the call of the people—and threaten the tenure of the Republican governor.

Jefferson's "spirit of resistance" was renewed. Teachers, snowplow drivers, sheriff's deputies, firefighters, students, small business owners, and retirees had demanded that their representatives join in that resistance to an elected despotism. And the senators who recognized that they were the people's servants, not their masters, responded.

On that February night when it was announced that the fourteen senators had halted the rush to enact the legislation

by the end of the week, tens of thousands of Wisconsinites celebrated the walkout by the Democratic senators, chanting
what was to become the credo of their movement: "This is
what democracy looks like."

Wisconsinites were employing "First Amendment remedies." And those remedies were working, perhaps imperfectly,
perhaps incompletely, but working still, as the founders intended.

The Constitution was a living document, the Bill of Rights
was a functioning force, more than two centuries after the ink
dried. The spirit of resistance was afoot in the city named for
the essential author of those documents, on the streets named
for the founders who joined him in advancing the American
experiment.

This James Madison would, most certainly, have approved.
Indeed, the most fretful of the founders might even have allowed himself to imagine that the experiment would survive
the battering it has taken from the elected despots and the
tyrannical factions he was so prescient to anticipate, so right
to fear, and so wise to guard against. It was Madison who in
1789 equipped patriots with the rights they would require to
challenge an elected despotism. And it was in Madison in 2011
that the tools were employed by the true descendants of the
generation of 1776, for whom a bill of rights was written not
as a protection but as a call to maintain the spirit of resistance
that has ever been America's greatest glory and surest hope.

CHAPTER 3

The Arc of History
Bends Toward Solidarity

How a Sense of Place
Shapes a Struggle, and a Future

If history is to be creative, to anticipate a possible future without denying the past, it should, I believe, emphasize new possibilities by disclosing those hidden episodes of the past when, even if in brief flashes, people showed their ability to resist, to join together, occasionally to win. I am supposing, or perhaps only hoping, that our future may be found in the past's fugitive moments of compassion rather than in its solid centuries of warfare.

—Howard Zinn, *A People's History of the United States*

No revolution vanishes without effect.

—Rebecca Solnit, March 2011

WHAT WOULD BOB DO?

—protest sign, hung around the statue of
Robert M. La Follette in Wisconsin's capitol, February 2011

GOVERNOR WALKER did not count on Sarah Roberts or the power that family connection, pride, and memory would play in the shaping of the militant movement that would eventually bring hundreds of thousands of public employees, teachers, students, and their allies to the great square that surrounds the state capitol in Madison. But when I met Roberts before one of the first great demonstrations outside the capitol, I knew Walker was in big trouble. And I knew that the key to the future, not just of the labor movement but of social-justice activism in America, was to be found with people like the young woman who was sitting in the Ancora coffee shop warming up.

With her blunt-cut blond hair and hip retro glasses, the library sciences grad student looked the picture of urban cool, except perhaps for the decades-old factory ID badge bearing the image of a young man. "A few weeks ago I asked my mom, 'What made my grandfather such a civic-minded man? Why was he always there to help someone who had lost their job? Take food to someone who couldn't make ends meet? Serve on the city council? What made him so incredibly engaged with his community and his state?' Mom looked at me and she said, 'Labor.'"

So it was that the granddaughter of Willard Roberts—a forty-five-year employee and proud union man at the Monarch Range plant in the factory town of Beaver Dam—pulled out her grandpa's ID and pinned it to her jacket when she learned that Walker was proposing to strip state, county, and municipal employees and teachers of their collective bargaining rights. "This state was built by people like him; this *country* was built by people like him. I think we all kind of forgot that until the governor woke us up," she said. "Walker thought he could bust the unions, privatize everything, give it all away to the corporations. But that was a great misfire. Because when he attacked the unions, he reminded us where we came from. We're the children and grandchildren of union workers and farmers and shopkeepers. That goes deeper, way deeper, than politics. This legislation is an affront to my whole family history."

After three decades of attacks on public sector unions, dating back at least to Ronald Reagan's breaking of the air traffic controllers in 1981, the mass uprising against Governor Walker's action revealed a popular understanding of the necessity of the labor movement that is far richer than even the most optimistic organizer imagined. The bonds are not just economic or political; they are emotional and personal. And when the determination of corporate interests and their political pawns to destroy unions—not by slow cuts, as is so often the case, but all at once—is revealed, all that talk of building coalitions, of creating movements linking union members with those who have never joined, suddenly moves from theory to practice. Thousands of students show up for an impromptu show by rocker Tom Morello and pump their fists in the air as they shout the lyrics of union songs they are only just learning. Tens of thousands of citizens—not just public workers fearing for their livelihoods but students fearing for their future and small-business owners fearing for their communities—chant in unison as they rally in cities across the state, "An injury to one is an injury to all."

After we finished talking on that Friday in February 2011, Sarah Roberts told me she couldn't go to the demonstration just yet: "I'm meeting my mom here. She's driving in. She wanted to be here to honor her father and to stand on the side of the workers."

★ ★ ★

THE REMARKABLE events that transpired in Wisconsin after February 11, 2011, when Governor Walker announced he would use a minor budget repair bill to strip away the rights of public employees and teachers to organize in the workplace and to engage in meaningful collective bargaining, made Wisconsin, in the words of American Federation of State, County & Municipal Employees (AFSCME) union president Gerald McEntee, "Ground zero in the fight for labor rights in the United States." They also created what Rev. Jesse Jackson, who rallied more than fifty thousand demonstrators on a freezing Friday night, described as "a King moment" for supporters of economic and social justice. The size of the demonstrations, which filled the central square of this capital city in much the way that demonstrators had filled Tahrir Square in Cairo just weeks earlier, focused more attention on an American labor struggle than has been seen in decades. This struggle—with its legislative disappointments, legal challenges and dramatic electoral twists and turns—renewed an ancient faith that mass movements can forge not only a new and better economy but a new and better politics. Walker secured some initial victories on some issues—too many issues.

But that was not the most important story out of Wisconsin. The most vital story was the one that people on both sides of this struggle least expected: after years of efforts by unions to rebrand and reposition themselves as "partners" and "constructive collaborators" with employers, the great mass of Americans still recognized that the most important role of the labor movement is as a countervailing force not just in the workplace but in politics. This was the crucial message, the crucial realization from Wisconsin. And it came at precisely the point when people needed it most: a time when public services and education are under constant assault from corporate privatizers and billionaire political donors who are more than ready to "invest" in election results that will lower their taxes and serve their business interests.

The watchword in Wisconsin was, and is, "solidarity." The symbol of the movement, a map of the state with its northern edges forming the clenched fist salute of union struggles since the Industrial Workers of the World raised it a century ago, sent the signal. And when once-cautious labor leaders and Democratic politicians saw tens of thousands of fists in the air at rallies in Madison and other communities across the state in February 2011, they began, tentatively at first but eventually with gusto, to embrace the symbolism and the language not just of militant labor but of a broader struggle for economic and social justice. That struggle was dramatically more open and inclusive than labor fights had tended to be, although it borrowed well and wisely from the 1999 protests in Seattle against the World Trade Organization. Slogans ("This Is What Democracy Looks Like!" and "The Whole World Is Watching!") and tactics (ongoing street protests, occupations of key spaces, civil disobedience, and outreach across what had previously been seen as lines of division) from Seattle provided reference points and inspiration for the Wisconsin protests. Key organizers who had been in Seattle—Ben Manski of the Liberty Tree Foundation and the Wisconsin Wave movement, Mary Bottari of Public Citizen and more recently the Center for Media and Democracy, and a generation of activists who had entered the labor movement following the WTO protests—were on the ground from the start in Madison. And they brought not just language and strategies but a set of values to the anti-austerity protests of a new movement. First and foremost among these was a faith in the power of broad coalitions. And nothing says coalition like a farmer in the thick of a labor struggle.

★ ★ ★

MY FRIEND Joel Greeno, a dairy farmer who hails from the same region of western Wisconsin where my dad was born, finished his chores on the morning of Saturday, February 26, and drove his truck to Madison to join what for him was a fight not just about labor rights but about the whole question of whether working people were going to have any pull at all in what was looking less and less like a democracy and more and more like a corporate kleptocracy. "The big corporations are organized. They're in this fight with all the money in the world," he shouted above chants of "What's disgusting? Union-busting!" "The big-money guys, they know what it's all about: if they can take away the collective bargaining rights of unions, if they can shut them up politically, we're all finished. How are farmers going to organize and be heard? If this goes through, none of us stand a chance."

Governor Walker actually agreed with Greeno. It was clear from the beginning that Walker's initiative, backed by big-money TV ad campaigns and by such national conservative groups as the hedge-fund-managed Club for Growth and the Koch brothers–funded Americans for Prosperity facade, had more to do with politics than balancing budgets. His bill, like similarly motivated if not quite so draconian measures pro-posed by GOP governors in other states, used a fiscal challenge as an excuse to achieve a political end. The governor claimed that he needed to eliminate most collective bargaining rights in order to address shortfalls in revenues. But state representa-tive Mark Pocan, a Madison Democrat and former cochair of the powerful legislative Joint Finance Committee, argued from the start of the struggle in 2011 that "Wisconsin can balance its budget. We've actually dealt with more serious shortfalls. This isn't about revenue and spending. This is about finding an excuse to take away collective bargaining rights and to destroy unions as a political force."The governor disputed Pocan's claim, but Pocan pointed to a review by the nonpartisan Fiscal Bureau that suggested the state might have been able to end the year with a slight surplus if a tax dispute with Minnesota and issues regarding Medicaid payments were resolved. While Wisconsin faced a genuine shortfall, it was much smaller than the one former governor Jim Doyle and Democratic legislators sorted out two years earlier in cooperation with state employee unions.

Walker's real goal was always clear. How clear? Let's consider some context. A year before the governor took office in January 2011, after winning a relatively low-turnout fall election that also saw Republicans take charge of this recently blue state's Assembly and Senate, the U.S. Supreme Court's *Citizens United v. FEC* decision removed barriers to corporate spending in election campaigns. GOP candidates reaped tremendous benefits from that ruling, which cleared the way for former White House political czar Karl Rove and fellow operatives to spend hundreds of millions on federal and state races. The Republican Governors Association, having collected a $1 million check from billionaire right-wingers Charles and David Koch and smaller contributions from other corporate interests, invested at least $3.4 million in electing Walker. As Lisa Graves, who heads the Madison-based Center for Media and Democracy, noted, "Big money funneled by one of the richest men in America [David Koch] and one of the richest corporations in the world [Koch Industries] ... put controversial Wisconsin governor Scott Walker in office." Walker's debt to the Koch brothers, whose PAC donated $43,000 to his campaign, and other wealthy donors and corporate interests was highlighted in the governor's budget repair bill, which in addition to attacking unions outlined a plan to restructure state government so Walker could sell off power plants in no-bid deals to firms like Koch Industries, while restructuring state health-insurance programs so that tens of thousands of Wisconsinites would lose an alternative to for-profit coverage.

The Koch-Walker connection became a central issue of the Wisconsin uprising when the tape of a prank phone call, in which the governor can be heard talking over strategy with a blogger impersonating David Koch, was released to the public. On it, Walker talked about coordinating spending campaigns to shore up GOP legislators who might otherwise balk at backing the bill. But even more telling was the governor's repetition of the phrase "This is our moment." At one point, Walker recalled a dinner with cabinet members on the eve of his announcement of the anti-union push. "I said, you know, this may seem a little melodramatic, but thirty years ago, Ronald Reagan ... had one of the most defining moments of his political career, not just his presidency, when he fired the air traffic controllers," said Walker. "And, uh, I said, to me that moment was more important than just for labor relations or even the federal budget; that was the first crack in the Berlin Wall and the fall of Communism. ... And, uh, I said this may not have as broad of world implications, but in Wisconsin's history—little did I know how big it would be nationally—in Wisconsin's history, I said this is our moment, this is our time to change the course of history."

Walker certainly understood the stakes. Across the United States, but particularly in the swing states of the Great Lakes region and the upper Midwest, public employee unions like

AFSCME, the American Federation of Teachers, and affiliates of the National Education Association have for decades been more than labor organizations. They are the best-funded and most aggressive challengers to attempts by corporate interests and their political allies to promote privatization, to underfund schools, and to win elections. If unions in Northern states are disempowered—as they are in much of the South, where anti-labor "right to work" laws are the norm—a debate already warped by the overwhelming influence of corporate cash becomes dramatically narrower and even more deferential to elite donors and big business.

Progressives have been talking about these concerns for a long time. They have tried to create movements to push back, sometimes with success, sometimes not. The same goes for organized labor. So what was different about Wisconsin? And, more significant, what potential is there to build a movement that extends far beyond one state?

★ ★ ★

THERE WAS NEVER any question that trade unionism has deep roots in the state of Wisconsin, especially public-sector trade unionism. It was in Wisconsin that the forerunner to AFSCME was founded in 1932 and that pioneering labor laws were enacted, including the first state law allowing local government workers and teachers to engage in collective bargaining, signed by Governor Gaylord Nelson in 1959.

Fifty-two years later, Nelson would become a touchstone figure in the framing of the 2011 struggle for Wisconsinites.

Before the first of the evening rallies where public employees and their allies would mass in ever-expanding numbers to protest against Governor Walker's plan, I went through one of three boxes of historic campaign buttons in my basement.

Finally, in the third box, I found it: a big white badge with blue lettering that read GAYLORD NELSON FOR GOVERNOR.

I pinned it on and headed to the rally, where, to my delight, people got the point: the right-wing Republican who now held the governorship was attacking more than just labor rights. He was attacking everything—and everyone—that forward-looking Wisconsinites valued.

Nelson, who as a U.S. senator in 1969 issued the call for the first Earth Day and ushered in an era of mass mobilization on behalf of environmental causes, was a Wisconsin progressive. His dad was a friend and supporter of Robert M. La Follette, the legendary progressive governor and senator. Nelson was a member of the small band of young progressives who took over the dormant Democratic Party in the late 1940s and turned it into a fighting liberal movement that swept state elections in 1958 and installed him as governor. Within months of that election, Nelson signed the pioneering collective bargaining law that extended protections to public employees across the state, precisely the law that Walker was seeking to eviscerate.

An understanding of these connections, both historical and personal, was at the heart of the uprising in Wisconsin that captivated, engaged, and inspired progressives across the nation during the first months of 2011 and that provided so much inspiration for the Occupy Wall Street movement. This ought not come as too much of a surprise. As historian Howard Zinn so frequently reminded us, it is impossible to explain what has happened in a particular struggle, and what might happen in other states, without embracing and exploring a past that serves always as prologue.

The question of "Why Wisconsin?" became a common one among activists, academics, and pundits trying to explain the scope and intensity of the reaction to Walker's proposal, a proposal that had taken just about everyone, including Wisconsin's savviest pols and pundits, by surprise. It's an appropriate inquiry, as the mass mobilization of union members, farmers, students, public employees, and private-sector workers countered a national narrative that had said the political energy in the country was on the right, that taxpayers see state and local employees and teachers as rampaging hordes emptying the public treasury, that unions are dead or dying, that sustained demonstrations happen only in Cairo and other Middle Eastern capitals, that nothing will rouse the great mass of Americans against corporate power.

Wisconsin proved different. Demonstrations so large that cameras could not capture their size and spirit embraced and amplified the language of the left with hundreds of thousands of people chanting, "An Injury to One Is an Injury to All!" "Tax the Rich!" "People Power, Not Corporate Power!" and "This Is What Democracy Looks Like!" Michael Moore captured the excitement of the moment when he recounted the failed efforts to generate a movement against bank bailouts and corporate welfare. "The executives in the board rooms and hedge funds could not contain their laughter, their glee, and within three months they were writing each other huge bonus checks and marveling at how perfectly they had played a nation full of suckers," he said. "Millions lost their jobs anyway, and millions lost their homes. But there was no revolt . . . until now!"

"On Wisconsin!" Moore shouted on a frigid Saturday in Madison. And fifty thousand people shouted back, "On Wisconsin!"

Time has taught us that the Wisconsin uprising was more than a freak phenomenon or a brief deviation from the steady race to the bottom politically. It was a turning point of national consequence. Of course, it was a lucky break that the vast right-wing conspiracy decided to pick a fight in Madison. The city, a university and state-government town, was a hotbed of 1960s protests and has remained a center of activism and independent media. People got information from classic mainstream media, including the proudly progressive *Capital Times* newspaper, which backed the struggle from the start, and from a solid local weekly, *Isthmus*. They could rely, as well, on vibrant community stations like WORT-FM, progressive commercial radio hosts like John "Sly" Sylvester, local stations that regularly broadcast progressive TV and radio hosts like MSNBC's Ed Schultz and Rachel Maddow, *Democracy Now!*'s Amy Goodman, and syndicated talker Thom Hartmann. Madison's local elected officials tended to be progressive and pro-union; Dane County sheriff Dave Mahoney played a critical role in easing tensions at the capitol, making it possible for demonstrators to maintain a sleep-in after the governor and GOP legislators tried to force them out. That infuriated Walker so much that he and legislative allies initiated a clampdown limiting access to the capitol before a judge ordered its reopening. Mahoney countered the governor's authoritarian impulses with repeated declarations that his deputies weren't "palace guards."

Local labor leaders were bold and flexible, far more militant in their thinking and tactics than is the norm nationally. University of Wisconsin students who were active in the world's oldest union of graduate employees, the Teaching Assistants' Association (TAA)—an affiliate of the American Federation of Teachers, which passionately and effectively embraced the Wisconsin struggle—were among the first to start sleeping at the capitol, and they were not isolated from the broader labor movement. Indeed, the immediate former president of the state

AFL-CIO, David Newby, had gotten his start with the TAA. So it was that a student protest was noted by and provided inspiration for the highest-ranking leaders in the labor movement. The same went for the decision by members of Madison Teachers Inc. (MTI), the city's education union, to take four days off to march and lobby against the bill. When Walker tried to set police and firefighter unions against the broader movement by exempting them from the worst assaults on labor rights, MTI's John Matthews immediately went to Firefighters Local 311 president Joe Conway Jr. and invited them to join the protest in solidarity; the initiative was so successful that firefighter and police union members became key players in the Wisconsin struggle and labor fights in states such as Ohio and Michigan. When the teachers went back to school after several days on the picket lines, parents and private-sector union members stepped into their places. When Walker tried to portray the unions and their members as greedy, union leaders made the not wholly popular choice to concede on a host of economic issues so the focus would remain squarely on the fight to keep collective bargaining rights. When Walker claimed that the demonstrators were being bused in from out of state, marchers began carrying signs naming the towns, villages, and counties they came from; many state and local employees showed up in their work uniforms. The international union leaders like AFT's Randi Weingarten and Leo Gerard of the United Steelworkers certainly provided tactical and economic support, but they did so with an awareness that people on the ground in Madison knew what they were doing and that, without pressure from focus groups, pollsters or D.C. "messaging" gurus, they had struck a chord not just in Wisconsin but nationally.

The militancy of the Wisconsin movement was exciting. It was inspiring. And that inspiration spread quickly to Florida,

Indiana, Maine, Michigan, Ohio, and other states targeted by Republican wrecking crew governors and legislators—and, it's worth noting, several Democratic governors or legislatures— who were racing to dismantle worker rights, public services, public education, and local democracy. The inspiration was certainly seen in the fall of 2011, as the Occupy Wall Street movement went to the belly of the beast, Manhattan's financial district, with a message and tactics that borrowed from and extended upon the Wisconsin model. Dozens of Wisconsinites were among the initial protesters on Wall Street. They brought ideas, values, but not a tight template.

That's the critical lesson.

For movements to achieve the scope and force of the Wisconsin uprising, it is important to understand the indigenous character of the revolt in Madison, Milwaukee, Platteville, Portage, Ashland, and Appleton. And it is essential for activists in every state to rediscover and honor their own homegrown progressive histories.

What happened in Wisconsin in the late winter and early spring of 2011 was not just a reaction against the dishonest and disreputable austerity agenda of old right-wing think tanks and new right-wing politicians. Nor was it merely an appropriate and necessary response to the overreach of a particular Republican governor. It had roots in Wisconsin, the state where the *Progressive* magazine was founded more than a century ago (as *La Follette's Weekly*) and continues to publish from an office just blocks from the epicenter of demonstrations that regularly drew tens of thousands of people to the great square surrounding the state capitol in Madison. Wisconsin has a rich history of progressive populist activism that stretches back to before the Civil War. The notion of resisting political and economic power is not new to the people of this state. Many of the mass demonstrations at the capitol were held on a corner of the square where stands a statue of Hans Christian Heg, the Norwegian immigrant who in the 1850s organized the "Wide Awakes," a militia that prevented fugitive slave catchers from operating in the state. Heg led a unit of "Norsemen" in the Civil War, and he died from wounds suffered at the Battle of Chickamauga. The Wisconsinites who returned from what they saw as "the noblest cause" carried with them an outsized sense of the state's responsibility to see off threats to a vision of a just and equitable United States.

Robert M. La Follette imbibed this worldview as a child; he was nurtured in rural Primrose Township on stories of courageous struggle not just against Southern slaveholders but the economic interests that would impose another form of bondage on the great mass of American farmers, shopkeepers, and workers. There was no lack of clarity and no confusion regarding the lines of battle. La Follette's political career, one of the most storied in American history, was a response to a call he heard issued in 1873 from Edward Ryan, the fiery chief justice of the Wisconsin Supreme Court, who warned:

> There is looming up a new and dark power....The enterprises of the country are aggregating vast corporate combinations of unexampled capital, boldly marching, not for economical conquests only, but for political power....The question will arise and arise in your day, though perhaps not fully in mine: "Which shall rule, wealth or man? Which shall lead, money or intellect? Who shall fill public stations, educated and patriotic freemen, or the feudal serfs of corporate capital?"

When I read Ryan's words to tens of thousands of Wisconsinites as they rallied at the capitol on a cold February night, many in the crowd were familiar with the words. They had studied them in history classes. They had heard them repeated from the stages of Fighting Bob Fest, an annual gathering—held for years in rural Baraboo, Wisconsin, and more recently in Madison—where as many as ten thousand progressives come together each summer to celebrate the legacy of La Follette and the radical reformers of a previous century. They had listened to variations on the theme in the speeches of former Democratic gubernatorial nominee Ed Garvey, former senator Russ Feingold, former House Appropriations Committee chair Dave Obey, current congresswomen Tammy Baldwin and Gwen Moore, state senators Mark Miller, Fred Risser, and Lena Taylor, and state representatives Mark Pocan and Cory Mason, all proud heirs to the progressive tradition.

Few states have done so fine a job as Wisconsin when it comes to retaining a sense of a distinct radical history.

So when the crowd on that February night was reminded of Chief Justice Ryan's words, the assembled masses spontaneously responded, "People power, not corporate power!"

The radical character of Wisconsin progressivism is part of a distinct Upper Midwest brand of activism that gave rise to the Minnesota Farmer-Labor Party and the North Dakota Nonpartisan League. From 1910 to 1960, Milwaukee repeatedly elected socialist mayors and congressional representatives, which explains why, in Wisconsin, "socialism" never became the epithet that it is in so much of our current political discourse.

There were setbacks along the way. Robert M. La Follette Jr., a great champion of labor rights, lost his U.S. Senate seat in a 1946 Republican primary to Joe McCarthy, and the late 1940s and early 1950s were a time of Republican hegemony in Wisconsin, a time when old progressives worried their movement had died.

Yet, in 1957, McCarthy's seat was won by Bill Proxmire, the first Democrat to represent Wisconsin in the U.S. Senate in a quarter century. A year later, the progressive movement re-emerged in a Democratic sweep of state offices. This was Gaylord Nelson's moment, and he grabbed it by working with Democratic legislators to enact a slew of pro-labor laws.

Nelson would go to the Senate in 1963 and spend the next eighteen years maintaining the progressive tradition of supporting civil rights and labor rights, promoting conservation and food and drug safety, and opposing military adventurism and the imperial presidency. When the streets of Madison exploded in the 1960s and early 1970s with anti-war demonstrations that were among the largest and most intense in that era of large and intense protests, Nelson was one of the few political figures who retained the respect of students who had lost faith in most political figures. At the same time, he was repeatedly reelected with support from blue-collar workers who appreciated his advocacy for organized labor, from farmers who saw him as a champion for small producers, from consumers who delighted in the scrutiny he brought to corporate abuses during a decade-long set of hearings on food and drug contamination. Only when the last of his reelection runs coincided with the Reagan Republican landslide of 1980 did Nelson lose his seat—a result that, while frustrating to progressives, provided a reminder that he had won repeatedly not in a deep-blue liberal state but in a purple-populist state that can and does follow at least some of the swings that characterize our national politics.

Twelve years later, Nelson's old seat was won back by the son of a Progressive Party stalwart, a young Democrat named Russ Feingold. Like Nelson, Feingold never really served as a national Democrat; he was an outlier, truer to the Wisconsin progressive populist tradition than to the compromised and compromising approach of Democratic presidents and congressional leaders. It was a point of honor that he was ranked the least popular senator among corporate lobbyists; this, Feingold said, was as La Follette intended. Unfortunately, as U.S. politics "nationalized" in 2010, after corporate interests faked up the faux populism of a Tea Party movement and turned disdain toward Barack Obama into an excuse for defeating all candidates with a "D" after their name, Feingold lost his reelection run in the same election that put Scott Walker in the governor's office.

Walker made a point of being sworn in on the opposite side of the capitol from the bust of Robert M. La Follette, where previous governors—Democrats and Republicans— had taken their oaths. That should have been a sign of what was coming. It was not just that Walker wanted nothing to do with the La Follette name and the progressive tradition; he was hoping that the bonds Wisconsinites felt with their state's history had frayed sufficiently so that he could lurch the state rightward.

But as soon as Wisconsinites began to occupy the state capitol during a remarkable demonstration of the people-power nature of the protests, students from the University of Wisconsin and AFSCME road crews surrounded the La Follette bust and made it the emotional and physical center of the occupation. Day after day, visitors to the capitol placed flowers in front of the bust. Quotes from La Follette were attached to the great pedestal on which it sat.

"We're guarding Bob and everything that's real about Wisconsin," declared Ed Sadlowski Jr., an AFSCME organizer from Rock County, who slept a dozen nights beside the bust. "This goes deep, man. This is about defending who we are.

Walker doesn't just want to take away collective bargaining. He wants to take our history as a state that stood on the side of the working people, not the corporations. We're not going to let him."

That understanding is essential to the spread of uprisings and movements like the one that developed in Wisconsin—where, months after the governor announced his anti-labor initiative, implementation of the measure continued to be blocked by legal actions, legislative maneuvers, and mass protests so large and consistent that the Republican majority leader of the Wisconsin state senate admitted in the spring of 2011 that many of his caucus members feared moving forward in the face of such opposition.

★ ★ ★

MAKE NO MISTAKE. What is often referred to simply as "Wisconsin" has spread. And it will continue to spread if activists in other states go to their own histories for inspiration.

Making these historical and emotional connections is essential to building popular movements that burst the boundaries of recent political coalition building. People have to feel that they have a stake in defending something bigger, something that is hardwired into their understandings of themselves as individuals and as citizens of a particular state. In an age of increasing homogenization of our politics, these connections form a vital—and too frequently undervalued—counterweight to a dumbed-down discourse.

It would be absurd to try and rally a radical movement in Massachusetts without recalling Sam Adams, Lexington, and Concord and the real tea party's anti-corporate message. That's a touchstone, a source of pride worth tapping into.

But every state has radical roots.

Michael Moore, a son of Flint, will remind you of just how much it matters that Michigan has a great labor tradition of sit-down strikes and United Auto Workers fights not just for union recognition and contracts but also for civil rights.

It matters that Montana was a hotbed of Wobbly activism in the days when the Industrial Workers of the World were on the march, and that towns such as Butte still identify with their radical labor history. And it matters that La Follette's running mate on the 1924 Progressive Party presidential ticket was Montana's anti-imperialist senator Burton K. Wheeler.

It matters that North Dakota Nonpartisan Leaguers started a state bank and state grain elevators almost a century ago, and that they are still going strong.

It matters that labor political activism in New York City didn't begin in the 1930s but in the 1830s, and that those first great fights put a woman, Fanny Wright, in the forefront. It matters that the Triangle Shirtwaist fire inspired so much of the passion not just for compensation and benefits but for human dignity that has underpinned what is best about the modern labor movement; and it matters that, when the one hundredth anniversary of the fire was celebrated in Union Square in late March of 2011, Wisconsin Education Association Council president Mary Bell was there to recognize the arc of history that still bends toward justice.

The histories of farm activism in Missouri, Kansas, and eastern Colorado are justifiably sources of great pride, and the fodder for contemporary organizing.

California did not start experimenting with radical politics in the 1960s; it began fifty years earlier with the radical governorship of Hiram Johnson—who went on to become one of La Follette's Senate allies in the struggle against imperialism and military profiteering—and the even more radical campaigning of Upton Sinclair and his "End Poverty in California" movement of the 1930s.

Connecticut has a rich socialist history in Bridgeport.

Pennsylvania has one in Reading.

Ohio has one in Cleveland and Toledo.

And so it goes.

The history is there, and it is powerful; it reminds people that they are part of something bigger, something stronger than a momentary battle. It creates a sense of connection with fellow workers but also with a legacy worthy of defending. Wisconsin's Fighting Bob Fest, the annual gathering of progressive faithful organized by Ed Garvey and his comrades, has always done this. And the Bob Fest model is ripe for export. "I'm here to thank you," Vermont senator Bernie Sanders told the Bob Fest crowd in September of 2011. "But," he added, "I am also here to say that we have to take this spirit to every state in the nation."

Sanders is correct.

In every state, we need to reclaim our progressive history, honor this heritage, and celebrate its continual life. There should be yearly progressive festivals in each state to invoke unique collective progressive memories. At these festivals, people gain strength by gathering en masse, recharging their batteries, reclaiming their roots—and they have fun doing it. Jim Hightower, an annual attendee at Wisconsin's Fighting Bob Fest, is a huge fan of the right to assemble not just to protest but also to celebrate who we are at events that "excite and empower ordinary people." So is Barbara Ehrenreich, a democratic socialist daughter of radical Butte, who authored the brilliant 2007 book on collective connection: *Dancing in the Streets: A History of Collective Joy*, in which she writes: "The empowerment comes from sensing that we are a part of something constant and strong. Maintaining an understanding of progressive roots, of where we come from—not for purposes of nostalgia but for renewal and revitalization—is a powerful tool."

That's what Wisconsinites did long before Scott Walker started going after unions, public schools, and public services. And this keeping of the faith is a part—a big part—of the answer to the question, "Why Wisconsin?"

It also explains why Wisconsin matters.

Wisconsin's history and progressive infrastructure created a sense, expressed by many in the state, that was perhaps best summed up by an instructor at Madison Area Technical College, Mary Bartholomew, who declared in February of 2011, "I'm so glad it came here first. But I know it's going to have to go everywhere."

It is easy to demonize a Scott Walker. Easy to imagine that one governor is the worst, that one moment is distinct. But, in the context of austerity struggles, Wisconsin is anything but unique. At the same time that Wisconsinites were battling over a "budget repair bill," at least forty-five other states and the federal government were wrestling with budget shortfalls and debt and deficit debates that by the summer of 2011 had come to dominate the national media to such an extent that nothing else seemed to matter.

It was clear in Wisconsin that the state's fiscal "crisis" was manufactured by Governor Walker and his allies for political gain. But nothing about this was distinct to Wisconsin. Even when fiscal problems are real, the answers offered by Republican governors like Walker—and Republican presidential candidates—are not. One of the most popular signs on the streets in Wisconsin, distributed by National Nurses United, declared BLAME WALL STREET. Instead of concessions, the nurses argued, it was time to focus on the corporate CEOs and speculators; as they point out, "In U.S. states facing a budget shortfall, revenues from corporate taxes have declined $2.5 billion in the last year. In Wisconsin, two-thirds of corporations pay no taxes, and the share of state revenue from corporate taxes has fallen by half since 1981." The same is true in other states, and nationally. These facts must be stressed, repeatedly and aggressively—as has already been done in the most serious of the state-based struggles and many of the manifestations of the Occupy Wall Street movement—if the debate is going to shift from cuts in public services and education to demands for fair taxes and the revenues necessary for services and schools.

For all the excitement generated by the uprising in Wisconsin, for all the hope the protests generated, the champions of economic democracy—as opposed to failed neoliberal dogmas, crude austerity, and the continual redistribution of the wealth upward—are still only at a point where we can talk about changing the terms of the debate. But this is a big deal. As we have seen, after the policy compromises of 2009 and the electoral setbacks of 2010, which were so disappointing to progressives, the upsurge in Wisconsin inspired people so powerfully that national labor leaders like Steelworkers president Gerard were ecstatic as they addressed the crowds of students, young teachers, and state employees at the capitol. "You have inspired this fat old white guy!" Gerard shouted to the crowds in Madison. He would say much the same thing months later, as the Steelworkers became one of the first major unions to embrace "Occupy Wall Street."

But it's not just the labor leaders who, after so many decades of trying to build mass movements on behalf of worker rights, were inspired. It was also people who had never aspired to be labor leaders; people whose connections with the labor movement had until February of 2011 been maintained by threads of personal history rather than contemporary experience.

This is about more than Wisconsin. Wisconsin merely provided a sense of the possible. This is about what matters far beyond the borders of one state. Indeed, this is about an arc-of-history movement that has the potential to transform America by pulling in all the disparate and previously disconnected individuals and communities that can form a grand coalition for economic and social justice.

It may have been family connection, pride, and memory that brought Sarah Roberts to the demonstrations in Madison. But on that frigid day that we met in that Madison coffee shop, she was not looking backward. Sarah Roberts was going forward.

"Something about this has struck a chord of fairness and humanity that runs deep in all of us," she explained to me. "We've been pushed around for so long, told we didn't have any power for so long. But I think our grandparents and our parents, they planted something in us, some values. And if we get pushed too far, we are going to push back. I think it started here, and I am so excited to see where we take it."

CHAPTER 4

"Wisconsin Is Not Broke, America Is Not Broke"

An Economics Lesson from Michael Moore

The challenge remains. On the other side are formidable forces: money, political power, the major media. On our side are the people of the world and a power greater than money or weapons: the truth.

—Howard Zinn, *A Power Governments Cannot Suppress*, 2006

You have aroused the sleeping giant known as the working people of the United States of America. Right now the earth is shaking and the ground is shifting under the feet of those who are in charge. Your message has inspired people in all fifty states and that message is: we have had it!

—Michael Moore, Madison, Wisconsin, March 5, 2011

HEAL MAIN STREET! TAX WALL STREET!

—National Nurses United union poster,
Madison, Lansing, Columbus, Washington, 2011

Y OU WILL LIVE in the history books!" Michael Moore
shouted from the rotunda of the state capitol to Wisconsin workers, teachers, and their allies who had filled the building on the first Saturday in March to protest against Governor
Scott Walker's assault on public-sector unions and public services. Speaking without a microphone, in a voice that was worn
but enthusiastic after addressing tens of thousands of protesters
outside the capitol a half hour earlier, Moore told the crowd
inside, "You have inspired so many people. You have inspired
the whole country. I just had to come and thank you."

This was Moore's first visit to the capitol that had become
the focus of international media attention, a house of government that was suddenly, surprisingly, yet completely filled
not with the governors but with the governed. The reversal
of political fortunes delighted the filmmaker who had devoted his career to bringing political and economic elites
down a few notches while bringing the great mass of Americans up. As he entered the statehouse, Moore gleefully joined
the call and response that had become of a staple of the capitol protests:

"Whose house?"

"Our house!"

Famous people had come to the capitol during this fight.
AFL-CIO president Richard Trumka. Rage Against the Machine guitarist Tom Morello. Rev. Jesse Jackson. Actress Susan
Sarandon. But Moore was unexpected. He had decided to
make the trip just hours before hitting the ground. The impe-
tus for his journey came very late on a Friday night, after
watching Fox News's Bill O'Reilly and Sarah Palin trashing
him for suggesting, in the filmmaker's words, that "the money
the twenty-first-century rich have absconded with really isn't

theirs—and that a vast chunk of it should be taken away from them."

GRITtv's Laura Flanders and her team, which had taken up the Wisconsin story early and passionately, had recorded Moore's comments about what was happening in Madison during an interview in New York and ran them on their national network of stations and websites. Conservative media "watchdogs" grabbed the clip, fed it to Fox and for a week the flacks for America's billionaire boys club had been battering Moore for engaging in "class warfare" by suggesting, again in his words, "that the money that the rich have stolen (or not paid taxes on) belongs to the American people."

It was not just bloviating media stars and failed vice presidential candidates who were bashing Moore. "Drudge/Limbaugh/Beck and even Donald Trump went nuts, calling me names and suggesting I move to Cuba," he explained on that March Saturday. "So in the wee hours of yesterday morning I sat down to write an answer to them. By 3:00 A.M., it had turned into more of a manifesto of class war—or, I should say, a manifesto *against* the class war the rich have been conducting on the American people for the past thirty years. I read it aloud to myself to see how it sounded (trying not to wake anyone else in the apartment) and then—and this is why no one should be up at 3:00 A.M.—the crazy kicked in: I needed to get in the car and drive to Madison and give this speech."

Moore realized that a road trip might be out of the question, but a plane flight was an option.

"I went online to get directions and saw that there was no official big rally planned like the one they had last Saturday and will have again next Saturday. Just the normal ongoing demonstration and occupation of the state capitol that's been in process since February 12th [the day after Mubarak was overthrown in Egypt] to protest the Republican governor's move to kill the state's public unions," Moore explained.

So, it's three in the morning and I'm a thousand miles from Madison and I see that the open microphone for speakers starts at noon. Hmm. No time to drive from New York. I was off to the airport. I left a note on the kitchen table saying I'd be back at 9:00 P.M. Called a friend and asked him if he wanted to meet me at the Delta counter. Called the guy who manages my website, woke him up, and asked him to track down the coordinators in Madison and tell them I'm on my way and would like to say a few words if possible—"but tell them if they've got other plans or no room for me, I'll be happy just to stand there holding a sign and singing Solidarity Forever."

Moore was sincere. But he should have known better.

The creative force behind a series of films, from *Roger and Me* to *Sicko*, the agitator who had done more than any politician or pundit to open discussions about deindustrialization, economic inequality and, yes, class divisions in a country that was founded on a promise that "all men are created equal" was going to be the star of any day that he showed up to sing "Solidarity Forever."

The kids, always blunter than their elders, said as much.

"You're famous!" declared a pre-teen protester in the capitol.

"You're my hero!" chimed a college student.

"No," Moore responded, "you're my heroes."

"You, all of you, you are America's heroes," he shouted to the crowd of union activists and their supporters, many of whom had slept night after night in the capitol before finally being forced out by the governor's manipulations of the legislative process and building management. But they were back that Saturday morning. And they were there with Michael Moore.

"Thank you! Thank you!" chanted the Midwestern-nice protesters, as they had for every speaker who came from afar but seemed to "get" what this uprising in Wisconsin was, and is, all about.

Moore got it in a fundamental sense, the sense of having waited a very long time for some mass of citizens, somewhere in America, to say, "We have had it!"

A dream deferred long enough can give way, even in the most optimistic and hopeful of Americans, to cynicism and despair.

Three weeks before Moore found himself in the Wisconsin capitol on that Saturday afternoon, the "smart" bet was that the economic powers that be would score another victory, perhaps their greatest victory of recent years, in the progressive heartland of Wisconsin. Walker had not just proposed to strip state, county, and municipal workers, as well as teachers, of their collective bargaining rights. He was promoting a plan that would render the unions politically dysfunctional by making it dramatically more difficult for them to collect dues and by forcing them to reorganize themselves each year. Union leaders and members were in shock. This was the most aggressive assault on the free speech and freedom of association rights of working people Wisconsin had ever seen. And it was the beginning of a national push to undermine the political power of unions to such an extent that the balance would permanently tip toward corporations, which were freed by the Supreme Court's *Citizens United* ruling to spend whatever they like on the buying of election results.

It wasn't just the naive and disconnected punditocracy that imagined Walker was certain to win the day. Many of the governor's most ardent critics doubted that his move would stir much more than a moan of mixed indignation and resignation. Instead, the governor's overreach was met with something unprecedented in recent American history: a push back from working Americans that developed into a movement. That movement stalled Walker's initiative for days, then weeks and then months. It shifted the political calculus of one state and inspired a national uprising. Wisconsin, Moore argued when he arrived on that first Saturday in March of 2011, had "aroused a sleeping giant—the working people of the United States of America."

This is one of the most fundamental of the many reasons why Wisconsin matters. Working families were battered before Walker announced his plan. Working families will be battered no matter what happens in Wisconsin. Much, much change is needed—the renewal of manufacturing towns, the restoration of rural communities, the reestablishment of progressive taxation and accountability for banks and speculators to rebalance budgets and usher in an era when government works for the people rather than billionaire campaign contributors. All of what must be accomplished is at the other end of the arc of history that began to be bent in Wisconsin, that was bent a little further in Ohio, and that began to bend nationally when the Occupy Wall Street movement took off.

But it is certainly true that something fundamental shifted when Wisconsin pushed back. And Moore came to Madison because he recognized how precious the moment was, not just in a political sense, not just in an economic sense, but in an emotional and idealistic sense. It was possible to believe again.

What Wisconsin had provided was a response to the closing scene of Moore's 2009 documentary, *Capitalism: A Love
Story*. The film closes on one of the most poignant notes in
modern filmmaking. After Moore has gone to Wall Street to
try to get America's bailout money back, after he has marked
off a "crime scene" where hundreds of billions of tax dollars
were diverted to bail out the very banks and corporations that
caused the financial meltdown of 2008, he speaks to the
American people about how frustrating it is that such wrongdoing has not inspired an uprising on the part of working
Americans.

Moore recalls Franklin Roosevelt's "Economic Bill of
Rights," and details the nation's drift from FDR's faith that
America could be a just and democratic land, then he explains
how the hedge fund managers and CEOs got bailed out while
working Americans got layoffs and foreclosure notices. "I refuse to live in a country like this and I'm not leaving," he says.
"We live in the richest country in the world. We all deserve a
decent job, health care, a good education, a home to call our
own. We all deserve FDR's dream. It's a crime that we don't
have it. And we never will as long as we have a system that en-
riches the few at the expense of the many. Capitalism is an evil
and you cannot regulate evil. You have to eliminate it and re-
place it with something good for all people . . . and that something is called democracy."

That was the political point of Moore's film, but he finished
on what is actually a more profound note. Worn and worried,
he says, "You know, I can't really do this anymore unless those
of you who are watching in the theater want to join me. I
hope you will. And speed it up!"

It took the better part of two years. But on a blustery Saturday three weeks into the Wisconsin struggle, Michael Moore

stood before tens of thousands of public workers, teachers, farmers, students, and their allies who had come to hear him attack the lie that "America is broke" with the truth: "The country is awash in wealth and cash. It's just that it's not in your hands. It has been transferred, in the greatest heist in history, from the workers and consumers to the banks and the portfolios of the über-rich."

Moore was tapping into an understanding that Wisconsin's budget "crisis," and those playing out at the same time in state capitols across the country, was political rather than financial in nature.

While Governor Walker claimed that he needed to advance his draconian "budget repair bill"—with its sweeping assault on labor rights, structure changes that would allow for limiting access to the state's BadgerCare and SeniorCare health programs and a scheme to sell off state assets in no-bid deals—in order to deal with an epic shortfall, Wisconsin's Legislative Fiscal Bureau said different.

The Fiscal Bureau is a classic Wisconsin "good government" agency created in 1968 by a Republican governor, Warren Knowles, and a Republican-controlled legislature.

Knowles, a rural Republican who served three terms as one of the state's most popular governors, was a Wisconsin Republican of the old school. He was big on government efficiency and sound management. And, like his Republican and Democratic predecessors, he believed in the "Wisconsin idea" that it was possible to reduce political pressures on the governing process by putting professionals in charge of determining whether the books were balanced.

Knowles and his allies established the Fiscal Bureau as a nonpartisan agency that would provide honest budget numbers for state legislators and the whole of state government.

For decades, the bureau did just that, earning the respect of legislators from both parties, including a young Scott Walker, who frequently cited the agency's data when he served in the Assembly.

Less than a month before Walker announced that the budget "crisis" had forced him to crack down on public employees and their unions, a bureau memo reported that Wisconsin had a $121 million surplus through the remainder of the current fiscal year.

The state's fiscal house was not entirely in order. There was the matter of unsettled issues relating to a reciprocity payment due Minnesota. Rising health care and prison costs posed a challenge. So it was not assured that Wisconsin would end the year fully in the black. But with as many as forty-seven American states experiencing fiscal troubles in the aftermath of the 2008 meltdown of the nation's banking sector, and an ensuing spike in unemployment, Wisconsin was looking to be in good shape.

Some governors might have celebrated. Not Walker. He wanted a crisis.

So he made one. In fact, he scheduled it, informing Republican legislators, who in turn informed Democratic colleagues, that they had better be in the state in mid-February because despite the winter season things were going to "get hot."

Imagining a worst case scenario—that Wisconsin might experience a shortfall before the end of the fiscal year—Walker began intriguing soon after his election by a 52–46 margin in 2010's Republican "wave," to write a "budget repair bill" before the need for a repair had been established.

When Walker presented his 144-page measure in mid-February, Wisconsin had not reached the statutory trigger, roughly $188 million, that would have demanded a repair bill. And though it was not entirely unprecedented in the history of a state populated by frugal Norwegians and efficient Germans to see a repair bill develop before the statutory trigger was reached, Democratic legislators asked why Walker was rushing to address a crisis that did not yet exist. And why was he doing so with a bill that attacked labor unions and local democracy while massively extending his own authority over cabinet agencies and creating dozens of new positions to be filled by his political cronies?

The governor had no background in bookkeeping, no accounting certification, no MBA. He did not even have a college degree, having dropped out of Milwaukee's Marquette University to pursue a political career that saw him run in eighteen primary and general elections over the course of a twenty-year climb from state representative to Milwaukee county executive to governor. All those campaigns over all those years had taught Walker the grand lesson of electoral politics in a sound-bite age: it is more important to sound like you know what you are doing than to actually know. To that end, Walker developed the shirt-always-ironed, shoes-always-polished, smile-always-pasted-on-just-right demeanor of a middle manager who was hoping to get his own franchise. Walker leavened his hustler style with a measure of moral "purpose" that went down well not only with the religious-right voters he pursued with steady determination but with rural Wisconsinites who, despite the fact that Walker hailed from the state's most populous county (Milwaukee), saw something of the small-town striver in the man who began positioning himself for a gubernatorial run as a young legislator. The son of a Baptist preacher, Walker had learned to cloak his intense ambition with talk of "service" and "duty." After FBI agents raided the home of his top political appointee in the fall of 2011, after his press secretary took immunity in a "John Doe" investigation of political wrongdoing, Walker let it be known that his integrity ought not be questioned because he had been an Eagle Scout.

Like Bill Clinton, Walker cut his political teeth not in the real world of electoral wards and precincts but in the surreal faux government that was organized each year by the American Legion as "Boys State." Like Clinton, he went to "Boys Nation" and met the president who would serve as his inspiration and political touchstone. In Clinton's case, it was John F. Kennedy; in Walker's case, it was Ronald Reagan. Walker revered Reagan as a political and a governing role model, as was evident in the midst of the Wisconsin uprising, when the governor got on the phone with that caller he thought was one of the billionaire Koch brothers. Walker wasted little time in comparing himself with Reagan, going to great lengths to sustain the comparison during the extended conversation with a caller who was in reality a lefty blogger, "The Buffalo Beast." The Beast's recording of Walker's soliloquy became an Internet phenomenon. In addition to the governor's Reagan obsession, the tape revealed a creepy, win-at-any-cost mentality, as Walker ruminated about how he and his aides had considered employing agent provocateurs to stir violence on the streets where peaceful demonstrations had drawn the elderly, children, and people with disabilities to protests against proposed cuts in state aid. Even Walker's most ardent critics were surprised by the extremes to which the governor was willing to go, and by his comment that his team rejected the idea of provoking violence only because they weren't sure how it would play politically. The Eagle Scouts do not give merit badges for false-flag violence, nor does their handbook entertain the calculus that says it's okay to create a circumstance where grandmothers with canes and kids in wheelchairs might be injured, so long as the tactic polls well.

So much for the whole "integrity" thing.

Walker's integrity was actually called into question long before the Koch call. From the start of the debate about whether it was necessary to "repair" the state budget, Walker played fast and loose with the numbers, to the detriment of the discourse and to the governor's reputation as a straight shooter, not to mention his math skills.

At the same time that he was supposedly fretting about where to find the money to pay public employees, maintain basic services, and fund education, the governor engineered the passage of roughly $140 million in new tax breaks for multinational corporations, which the Republican-controlled legislature dutifully passed and sent to his desk for signing in the weeks before the "crisis" hit. He also rejected more than $800 million in federal transportation funds that other states have rushed to get, in a move that scuttled a high-speed rail project and caused a Spanish train manufacturer that had been planning to locate a new factory in the Milwaukee area to quit Wisconsin. And in the very week that he was pushing his budget repair bill, the governor rejected almost $25 million in federal money to develop broadband wireless services in rural areas, which some of the state's least-populous counties had been seeking for years.

These moves, at a time when the state was supposedly experiencing a financial meltdown, begged the question, "Why?"

Even if there was a need to "repair" the budget, as Walker claimed, the legislature had a long history of addressing such challenges with minor spending and revenue adjustments. "We'd dealt with much bigger challenges than this more times than I can count," recalled Democratic state senator Fred Risser, the senior member of the legislature. A Madison Democrat who began serving in the capitol when Dwight Eisenhower was president, Risser explained that "budget repair bills aren't supposed to be policy measures. They're not supposed to change everything about how the state operates. They're supposed to make the adjustments that are needed before you get around to preparing the next budget. But here's Scott Walker, fresh from giving away all these tax breaks and turning down all this federal money, telling us that we have to pass the most radical legislation I've seen in my time in the legislature. It makes no sense."

Risser, a genteel eighty-four-year-old who was respected by members of both parties for his mild manners, was being a gentleman.

There was a popular answer to the "Why?" question. Walker's critics, including clean-government groups, charged that the governor was making budget decisions not with an eye toward fiscal responsibility but with an eye toward rewarding political benefactors. Out-of-state corporations, road-building interests that did not want competition from high-speed rail, and telecommunications corporations that wanted to cash in on the demand for broadband, these interests benefited from decisions made by Walker in the first weeks of his governorship. Then, feigning fear that the state was headed toward a crash, the governor declared that Wisconsin needed to scrap collective bargaining for public employees and teachers and alter the way in which the state operated.

Scot Ross, of the watchdog group One Wisconsin Now would eventually accuse Walker of surrendering Wisconsin to Wall Street and the corporate special interests that bought him the keys to the governor's mansion. State representative Mark

Pocan, the Madison Democrat who was the immediate former cochair of the legislature's Joint Finance Committee, said that the governor and his allies were giving "an awful lot of love to their corporate friends."

Those were harsh words for a newly minted governor.

But they made sense at a time when everything about Walker's economic construct was absurd.

On the one hand, the governor argued that the tax breaks he had developed for corporations would not be fully implemented until the next fiscal year. So, his apologists claimed, it would be wrong to accuse him of ginning up a crisis to achieve political ends. On the other hand, he was saying that he needed the most ambitious "budget repair bill" in Wisconsin history to address the challenges the state would face in, you guessed it, the next fiscal year.

As Nicholas Johnson, vice president for state fiscal policy with the Center on Budget and Policy Priorities, noted in a memo regarding the Wisconsin mess that he prepared for the *Washington Post*, "[In] a technical sense, the tax cuts didn't create the current-year shortfalls that in turn are creating the specific opening for the 'budget repair bill.' However, it is true that the tax cuts are worsening the state's overall budget picture, and it is the state's overall budget picture—not the current-year picture alone—that the [governor] is using to justify going after the workers."

Debates about budgeting are often complex. Lots of heads were spinning in Wisconsin in the first months of 2011. More important, the governor, his aides, and his media echo chamber (initially Milwaukee-area right-wing talk radio hosts such as Charlie Sykes and Mark Belling, but eventually national players such as Rush Limbaugh, Glenn Beck, and Sean Hannity) were spinning. It was easy to get confused.

So let's get down to some basics:

1. The Fiscal Bureau reported in January 2011 that Wisconsin had a $121.4 million surplus through the end of the fiscal year.

2. The state had an unresolved economic dispute with Minnesota and faced the threat of some potential spikes in health care and prison costs that could have required a budget repair bill. But the state had not reached the trigger point where such a bill would be necessary.

3. When, and if, the trigger point was reached, the wise counsel of Risser was well taken: "This is not a crisis. We've done budget repair bills before. We've always been able to sort these things out."

Risser was absolutely right. He was also right when he said, "We now know this struggle is not about the money. Public employee unions have offered many concessions to help solve the state's fiscal crisis. When those efforts at compromise were ignored, it became clear that Governor Walker and his allies are part of a national agenda, fueled by big-money conservative groups, to destroy the unions at all costs."

That's the bottom line: The Wisconsin dispute was never about the money. It was not a fiscal crisis. It was a political crisis. And Walker always had the power to resolve it by refocusing on fiscal issues, as opposed to pursuing the political goal of breaking unions.

It was that recognition of political chicanery and economic larceny that brought the crowds to the streets of Madison and other Wisconsin cities, and that would eventually draw Michael Moore to the rotunda of the capitol.

In the weeks before Moore arrived, the size of the crowds expanded at roughly the same rate as did the understanding that the fight in Wisconsin was a fundamental struggle between economic elites and the great mass of working Wisconsinites.

One week before the Saturday when Moore came to Madison, upward of 125,000 Wisconsinites rallied at the state capitol, as tens of thousands more gathered in communities across the state that national union leaders declared to be "ground-zero in the fight for labor rights, ground-zero in the fights for the American middle class."

Snow fell throughout the day on that February 26, and temperatures were frigid. It was so cold, in fact, that my farmer friend Joel Greeno could not get the tractor he had hoped to drive in the mass march around the capitol free from an ice pack. "So I just finished my chores and hopped in the truck so I could get here as soon as I could," Joel explained. "It would have killed me if I missed this. This is the most amazing thing I have ever seen happen in Wisconsin."

In interviews with national networks, Governor Walker tried to spin the fantasy that the crowds that had surrounded the capitol initially and then began sleeping inside was not made up of real Wisconsinites. That was a lie, coming from a politician who had spun a web of deception so obvious in its intents and bumbles that it was generating handmade signs that declared Walker GOVERNOR OF WALL STREET, NOT WISCONSIN.

Picking up the pay-to-play politics theme, hundreds of signs referenced the prank call with the Koch brother who wasn't a Koch brother. WALKER IS THE GOVERNOR OF KOCH-ONSIN, read one sign, while another announced WALKER HAS ONE CONSTITUENT: DAVID KOCH. And then there was GOVERNOR WALKER, YOUR KOCH DEALER IS ON LINE TWO.

While the February 26 rally in Madison saw the largest gathering up to that point of activists in what was rapidly becoming a mass movement for economic and social justice, they were joined that day by supporters in every one of the nation's state capital cities, as well as Washington, D.C. Thousands packed the grounds of government buildings in Denver, St. Paul, and Columbus, while even larger crowds were seen in San Francisco, Chicago, and New York.

Energized by the images of Wisconsinites filling their state capitol with chants of "What's disgusting? Union busting!" unions across the country recognized an opening that some of them had been seeking for years. And they used it to outline clear and uncompromising agendas for the particular defense of public services and the rights of workers but also for the broader economic fight that could neither be avoided nor denied.

After too many years on the losing end of a class war that was being waged by Wall Street and the big banks, it was time to fight back with something more than an austerity agenda of cut, cut, and then cut.

One of the strongest statements came from Rose Ann De-Moro, executive director of National Nurses United, the militant health care union that had a history of mass mobilization on behalf of labor rights and the public services that determine whether Americans live or die. DeMoro explained "what all working families should know."

The nurses' union boiled the economy debate down to core themes, as part of the experiment in popular education that began in Wisconsin and has now gone national; among those addressing the Occupy Wall Street crowd in Lower Manhattan late in September was Nobel Prize–winning economist Joseph Stiglitz.

DeMoro used questions and answers to explain the economics of the Wisconsin fight and to make a point:

- *Who caused the economic crisis?* Banks, Wall Street speculators, mortgage lenders, global corporations shifting jobs from the U.S. overseas.
- *Who is profiting in the recession?* Corporate profits, third quarter of 2010, were $1.6 trillion, 28 percent higher than the year before, the biggest one-year jump in history. Meanwhile, average wages and total wages have fallen for all incomes, except the wealthiest Americans whose income grew fivefold.
- *Who is not paying their fair share?* In U.S. states facing a budget shortfall, revenues from corporate taxes have declined $2.5 billion in the last year. In Wisconsin, two-thirds of corporations pay no taxes, and the share of state revenue from corporate taxes has fallen by half since 1981. Nationally, according to a General Accountability study out today, 72 percent of all foreign corporations and about 57 percent of U.S. companies doing business in the United States paid no federal income taxes for at least one year between 1998 and 2005.
- *Are public employees overpaid?* State workers typically earn 11 percent less and local public workers 12 percent less than private employees with comparable education and experience. Nationally, cutting the federal payroll in half would reduce spending by less than 3 percent.
- *Would pay and benefit concessions by public employees stop the demands?* The right has made it clear it wants (a) cuts in public pay, pensions, and health benefits, followed by (b) restricting collective bargaining for public sector workers, followed by (c) prohibiting public sector unions.

- *Will the right be troubled if cuts in working standards make it harder to recruit teachers and other public servants?* No. Take public teachers, many of whom have accepted wage freezes and other cuts in recent years. Many in the right have a fairly open goal of privatizing education, and destabilizing public schools serves this purpose. The right also salutes the shredding of government workforce, part of its overall goal to gut all government service and make it harder to crack down on corporate abuses or implement other public protections and services.
- *Will the right stop at curbing public workers' rights?* Employers across the United States are demanding major concessions from private-sector workers and breaking unions. Right-wing governors and state legislators are seeking new laws to restrict union rights for private and public employees.
- *Does everyone have a stake in this fight?* Yes. It's an old axiom that the rise in living standards for the middle class in the 1950s was the direct result of a record rate of unionization in America. It is of course unions that won the eight-hour day, weekends off, and many other standards all Americans take for granted, which are now often threatened with the three-decades-long attack on unions spurred by that right-wing icon Ronald Reagan. The corollary is that increased wages and guaranteed pensions put money into the economy, with a ripple effect that creates jobs and spurs the economy for all.

DeMoro and National Nurses United took the lead in national organizing, recognizing that the first lesson to be taken from Wisconsin was that "Working people—with our many allies, students, seniors, women's organizations, and more—are inspired and ready to fight."

This was what Michael Moore had been waiting for, pleading for, and a week after the mass mobilizations in Madison and state capitols across the country, the filmmaker arrived to confirm for the workers of Wisconsin that their instincts were right: America is not broke. It just has a broken set of priorities.

As Moore explained, with a combination of serious intent and schoolboy glee that is his unique contribution to the American discourse:

> Today, just four hundred Americans have more wealth than *half* of all Americans combined. Let me say that again. Four hundred obscenely rich people, most of whom benefited in some way from the multi-trillion dollar taxpayer "bailout" of 2008, now have as much loot, stock and property as the assets of 155 million Americans *combined*. If you can't bring yourself to call that a financial coup d'état, then you are simply not being honest about what you know in your heart to be true. And I can see why. For us to admit that we have let a small group of men abscond with and hoard the bulk of the wealth that runs our economy, would mean that we'd have to accept the humiliating acknowledgment that we have indeed surrendered our precious Democracy to the moneyed elite. Wall Street, the banks and the Fortune 500 now run this Republic—and, until this past month, the rest of us have felt completely helpless, unable to find a way to do anything about it.

Then Michael Moore let rip.

> I have nothing more than a high school degree. But back when I was in school, every student had to take one semester

of economics in order to graduate. And here's what I learned: Money doesn't grow on trees. It grows when we make things. It grows when we have good jobs with good wages that we use to buy the things we need and thus create more jobs. It grows when we provide an outstanding educational system that then grows a new generation of inventors, entrepreneurs, artists, scientists and thinkers who come up with the next great idea for the planet. And that new idea creates new jobs and that creates revenue for the state. But if those who have the most money don't pay their fair share of taxes, the state can't function. The schools can't produce the best and the brightest who will go on to create those jobs. If the wealthy get to keep most of their money, we have seen what they will do with it: recklessly gamble it on crazy Wall Street schemes and crash our economy. The crash they created cost us millions of jobs. That too caused a reduction in tax revenue. Everyone ended up suffering because of what the rich did.

The nation is not broke, my friends. Wisconsin is not broke. Saying that the country is broke is repeating a Big Lie. It's one of the three biggest lies of the decade: (1) America is broke, (2) Iraq had WMDs, and (3) The Packers can't win the Super Bowl without Brett Favre.

That was an applause line, especially with a crowd that held aloft green-and-gold signs with a map of their state and the words SUPER BOWL CHAMPIONS OF THE LABOR MOVEMENT.

But Michael Moore was going for a bigger applause line: the one that comes not from name-dropping a favorite team but from speaking truth to the power of the bankers, the speculators, and the corporate CEOs who would collapse a republic rather than sacrifice a single penny for the common good:

They have created a poison pill that they know you will never want to take. It is their version of mutually assured destruction. And when they threatened to release this weapon of mass economic annihilation in September of 2008, we blinked. As the economy and the stock market went into a tailspin, and the banks were caught conducting a worldwide Ponzi scheme, Wall Street issued this threat: either hand over trillions of dollars from the American taxpayers or we will crash this economy straight into the ground. Fork it over or it's goodbye savings accounts. Goodbye pensions. Goodbye United States Treasury. Goodbye jobs and homes and future. . . .

The executives in the board rooms and hedge funds could not contain their laughter, their glee, and within three months they were writing each other huge bonus checks and marveling at how perfectly they had played a nation full of suckers. Millions lost their jobs anyway, and millions lost their homes. But there was no revolt. Until now!

The look of delight on Moore's face when he uttered those words, and the knowing roar of approval from the crowd, was the most powerful moment on that Saturday, March 5, and one of the most powerful moments of the Wisconsin fight-back.

It was followed not by the poignant plea for engagement that closed *Capitalism: A Love Story* but rather by a celebration of the answer to that plea.

"On, Wisconsin!" Moore shouted. "Never has a Michigander been more happy to share a big, great lake with you! You have aroused the sleeping giant known as the working people of the United States of America. Right now the earth is shaking and the ground is shifting under the feet of those who are in charge. Your message has inspired people in all fifty states and that message is: *we have had it!*"

The crowd chanted, "We have had it! We have had it!"

Moore continued, "We reject anyone who tells us America is broke and broken. It's just the opposite! We are rich with talent and ideas and hard work and, yes, love. Love and compassion toward those who have, through no fault of their own, ended up as the least among us. But they still crave what we all crave: Our country back! Our democracy back! Our good name back! The United States of America. *Not* the Corporate States of America. The United States of America!"

"The United States of America!" came the response from the crowd, shouting the words with a sense of joy and satisfaction. "The United States of America!" "The United States of America!"

It was clear in that moment, that amazing moment, that the American story of submission and surrender was done. Now, finally, the American story—not just the Wisconsin story but the American story—of the fight for a republic that might yet realize FDR's dream of economic liberty had begun.

Michael Moore was not alone anymore in his refusal to live in an America defined and deranged by banksters and crooked CEOs. Tens of thousands, hundreds of thousands, millions of Americans were coming, as their ancestors had before them, to the village green, to the city hall, to the capitol square, to Wall Street and Washington, and declaring, "We refuse to live in a country like this and we're not leaving."

CHAPTER 5

The Next Media System

Beyond "Old" and "New," a Journalistic and Democratic Media for the Twenty-First Century

Revolutions create genius and talents; but those events do no more than bring them forward. There is existing in man, a mass of sense lying in a dormant state, and which, unless something excites it to action, will descend with him, in that condition, to the grave.

—Thomas Paine, *Rights of Man,* 1792

The revolution will not be televised, will not be televised, will not be televised. The revolution will be no rerun brothers. The revolution will be live.

—Gil Scott-Heron, *Small Talk at 125th and Lenox,* 1970

THE REVOLUTION IS BEING TELEVISED!

—protest sign, Madison, Wisconsin, February 2011

W HAT THE HECK is going on in Wisconsin?" Ed Schultz
asked me on February 14, the Monday after Governor
Walker moved to strip state, county, and municipal employees
and teachers of their collective bargaining rights. I had appeared
for years as a guest on Schultz's nationally syndicated radio show
and, more recently, on his MSNBC cable television program.
Usually, we ranted and raved about the high crimes and misde-
meanors of Dick Cheney, the foibles of Sarah Palin, or our
shared disappointment with Democrats who frequently forget
the lessons of Franklin Roosevelt and Harry Truman. But this
show was different. We weren't talking about what was happening in Washington, the city I have covered for years. We were
talking about what was happening in Madison, Wisconsin, the
city where my family had lived, on and off, since 1838. We were
talking about a right-wing governor's attack on organized labor,
about the broad political ramifications of the fight, and about
what this all meant for America's rapidly dwindling middle class.

More often than not, what passes for "mainstream media"
in America reaffirms Bruce Springsteen's "57 Channels (and
Nothing On)" calculus. But Schultz has always pushed the
limits in the right direction. And that certainly was the case
that Monday, as we talked about the rights of workers, the
value of public employees, and the necessity of unions to a
free and democratic society. This was not a depressing assessment of decline and degeneration, of missed opportunities and
cracked paradigms.

"I'm thinking that people aren't going to put up with that,"
he shouted. "Wisconsin's gonna push back, right?"

Right.

Walker's move to undermine collective bargaining rights
was about to do something that decades of organizing, cam-

paigning, and "messaging" by the labor movement had failed to do. With his dramatic overreach, the governor would force Wisconsinites to answer the question Florence Reece had raised eighty years earlier in the coal country of Kentucky's "Bloody Harlan," the essential question of every justice struggle: "Which side are you on?" And with their answer, they would open a discussion about the future of public-sector unions—and a whole lot more. That discussion would extend beyond the usual "fifteen minutes of fame" afforded most stories from outside the Beltway. The conversation lasted for weeks in much of the national media, and for months in the media (like Schultz's nationally syndicated radio show and his MSNBC program) that "got" what the Wisconsin fight was really about. Schultz understood, instinctively and immediately, that Walker's plan put a target on the American middle class. Manufacturing unions had already taken their hit; now, the same people who shipped our factory jobs overseas were coming for the public sector. His understanding was paralleled by another radio talker, Thom Hartmann, who for months would devote a portion of his show each day to placing the Wisconsin fight in the context of the corporate right's bigger and bolder national plan to undo the New Deal and restore the politics of a past where robber barons ruled and the range of options for Americans extended from monopoly to duopoly. Wisconsin's governor did not merely seek to weaken the organized opposition to his privatization-and-plunder policies—particularly the unions that might advocate for public services and public education—he sought to renew a spoils system where key posts in government were filled not with civil servants but with political cronies. By weakening the unions and century-old protections against the corruption of the commons, he was proposing one of the most radical transformations of the

American political landscape in seventy-five years, and he was not just proposing it for one state on the nation's northern tier. As his conversation with the caller he thought was billionaire David Koch revealed, Walker imagined himself as an epic change agent caught up in his very own "rendezvous with destiny" moment.

"This is our moment," Walker chirped. "This is our time to change the course of history."

This was a great story, a great American story, that had all the elements that any reporter, commentator, or anchor who retained even the barest fascination with the American journey could sink his or her teeth into. There was not just a naked power grab. There was, as well, the response. The amazing, unprecedented, epic response that would include an occupation of the state capitol lasting not for hours or days but for weeks; some of the largest pro-labor mobilizations since the 1930s and a movement to recall and remove errant officials that would shake the state's political moorings. The uprising was so out of character with recent American experience that it became an international news story that got commentators on the BBC, Al Jazeera and other networks speculating about the arrival of a new global activism that was spreading from Tripoli to Cairo to Benghazi to Madison. Everyone wanted a piece of it; the hosts of a Jamaican radio show called my cell phone every day to check on whether the crowds were still closing rallies singing Bob Marley's rebel call: "Get up! Stand up! Stand up for your rights!" (They were.) As they got the message that a mass movement was spreading from North Africa to North America, the crowds began to grow in cities and towns across Wisconsin, and then, suddenly, Facebook pages were featuring images of thousands of people surrounding capitols in Indianapolis, Columbus, Lansing. Eventually, the crowds would form on Wall Street itself, and outside the White House in Washington.

Ed Schultz recognized the epic character of the events that were unfolding. He came to Wisconsin to tell the story, not once or twice, but repeatedly. In February, when tens of thousands of protesters filled the streets of Madison, Schultz was surrounded by masses of cheering Wisconsinites as he hosted his show from a makeshift outdoor studio across from the capitol where thousands of students and union members were "sleeping in." The roar of the crowd and the energy of the moment created an electricity that made it possible to believe the message on a sign held aloft on one of those cold winter nights, a variation on the theme of the inimitable Gil Scott-Heron (who would pass away just three months later): THE REVOLUTION IS BEING TELEVISED.

Ed Schultz could not get enough of the struggle. When he wasn't in Wisconsin, Schultz hosted this writer, and Wisconsin legislators, union leaders, municipal workers, teachers, and citizens. His commitment, as a national cable television host, to cover a state-based labor struggle was unprecedented. "I'm not letting go of this story," Ed would tell me. "This may be happening in Wisconsin, but it doesn't stop there. It doesn't stop in Ohio. Or Michigan. Or Florida. This is the story of whether we're going to have a middle class in America."

Unfortunately, Ed's enthusiasm was most remarkable because few other cable or radio hosts with national reach, few reporters or writers or commentators—even from liberal-leaning and progressive media—would begin to approximate that commitment as the story was unfolding. Some never tried to get it right. In fact, the general mangling of the largest pro-labor protests in recent American history, protests that brought the streets around a state capitol to a standstill for weeks on end, prompted the analysis and advocacy group Media Matters to issue frequent comparisons of the national media's over-the-top coverage of tiny Tea Party events and their failure to note mass mobilizations by folks on the other side of the debate about debt, deficits, and austerity. Talking Points Memo's Josh Marshall, noting the disparity, suggested at one point that critics of the governor's proposals might want to bus in several thousand Tea Party activists so that they could get major media outlets to pay as much attention to the mass demonstrations in Madison as they did to small Tea Party gatherings.

Several months later, Media Matters' Eric Boehlert wrote, "I'm convinced that if the Tea Party had brought a state capital to a month-long standstill the way union supporters did in Wisconsin, CNN, for instance, would have built an on-site studio and provided constant, around-the-clock coverage of the political drama. By comparison, CNN's Wisconsin coverage was often perfunctory and the cable news channel too often ignored the grassroots nature of that political uprising."

Boehlert's assessment was astute, and appropriate. The protests in Wisconsin were so large that they demanded basic attention. But most major media outlets covered them with a "tarmac tap"—sending a crew in, keeping them on the ground just long enough to get the "Madison" dateline. While the events in Wisconsin drew more attention than any state-based labor struggle in decades, the coverage did not begin to approximate what was seen in the New Deal and Fair Deal eras, when the nation's newspapers and radio networks employed more than a thousand labor reporters and "industrial correspondents," and when the stories of the San Francisco general strike, the Flint sit-down strike, the bloody "Little Steel" fight, the rise of the CIO, A. Philip Randolph's "March on Washington" to integrate defense industrials, post-war

walkouts by autoworkers, coordinated bargaining by electrical workers, "Operation Dixie" southern organizing drives, Taft-Hartley, and the flexing of union political muscles to keep Harry Truman in the White House and to put allies like Wayne Morse and Paul Douglas in the Senate drew every bit as much attention as mergers and acquisitions, market fluctuations, and bank bailouts.

★ ★ ★

MEDIA THAT ONCE covered organized labor as an equivalent force in America's economic and political life has for years covered union activity as a footnote to the round-the-clock cheerleading of the business channels that keep telling retirees to gamble on the casino capitalism of the Dow, the S&P, and Nasdaq. Before the protests in Wisconsin broke out, decades of neglect had caused media managers, editors, and reporters to imagine that it was not just the "labor beat" but labor itself that had become a thing of the past. When pollsters asked, for the first time in years, about attitudes toward unions, business commentators were openly skeptical about results that showed that Americans recognized organized labor as a necessary counterbalance to corporate control over our economic and political life, that collective bargaining rights were cherished as essential liberties, that public employee and teacher unions were broadly respected, and that just about everyone outside Washington and the few blocks of southern Manhattan around Wall Street recognized that the real culprits in the "America's going broke" scenario were tax-dodging CEOs and bailed-out bankers—not the plow drivers who get up at 2:00 A.M. to clear two feet of snow from county highways or the teachers who use their own money to buy school supplies for disadvantaged kids. How could it be that Americans did not

hate unions and union members when Rush Limbaugh and Sean Hannity had for years been telling them to do so, with an unrelenting repetition not heard since the days when Soviet radio went off the air?

But Limbaugh and Hannity weren't really the problem. Their bias was evident and ideological. Far more frustrating were the supposedly mainstream outlets that cloaked their biases in claims of impartiality, shaving away the rough edges of a Hannity hit job and reaching pretty much the same conclusion—or, worse yet, imagining that there was no interest on the part of working Americans in the stories of, er, well, working Americans.

Laura Flanders, who got her start as a brilliant media critic with the watchdog group Fairness and Accuracy in Reporting (FAIR) and went on to become a brilliant media maker as the host of an Air America radio show and GRITtv, noted that the events in Madison played out just days after cable stars such as Anderson Cooper had been delivering reports from Egypt so breathless that viewers could see the anchorman's chest heaving beneath his famously tight T-shirt. "The comparison between Cairo and Madison could not have been more stark," observed Flanders. "In Cairo, as the crowds grew, the media coverage increased. In Madison, as the crowds grew, it decreased."

So it was that, when the largest of the Wisconsin demonstrations took place on March 12, with an estimated 180,000 people massing at the capitol in Madison and tens of thousands more filling the streets of communities across the state, most major print, broadcast, and cable media had no reporters on the scene and neglected to report the breathtaking events of that Saturday in the Sunday papers or on the Sunday-morning

TV talk shows that had settled back into the comfortable con-
fines of their D.C. studios—and mentalities.

When he visited Madison a week earlier, Michael Moore,
as astute a media critic as there is, appealed to mainstream media
outlets to tell the whole story of what was happening in Wisconsin, and the broader story of a popular uprising against austerity measures that were as ill conceived as they were brutal.
"The media has done a poor job covering this (imagine a
takeover of the government HQ in any other country, free or
totalitarian—our media would be all over it)," Moore explained.
"But this one scares them and their masters—as it should."

Moore recognized the disconnect between what he saw
on the ground in Wisconsin—massive peaceful protests that
were every bit as inspiring as the popular protests abroad,
which had so recently attracted so much coverage from U.S.
newspapers and networks—and the generally disengaged response of the Washington press corps and the punditocracy to
a domestic uprising. As the protests in Wisconsin went "national," the few strengths and many pathologies of major media
in the United States were fully on display. In some cases, the
story was told well and wisely. The ever-vigilant Amy Goodman's *Democracy Now!* program was paying attention immediately; I was asked to record a commentary that aired within
hours of the first protests on the hundreds of radio and cable
television programs that make up Goodman's remarkable network of conscience. Within days, as the protests grew in size
and scope, and as it became clear that they were upsetting the
governor's agenda, Goodman brought her program to Madison, and boldly broadcast an hour-long show from inside the
occupied capitol, where she was literally surrounded by students who had slept through the night in hearing rooms

where Democratic legislators maintained round-the-clock sessions to record the opposition of the people of Wisconsin to the governor's proposal.

Ed Schultz arrived around the same time and did his national cable show from that street corner opposite the capitol, where he was surrounded night after night by a crowd that numbered in the thousands. MSNBC hosts such as Rachel Maddow picked up the theme and ran with it ably. Slowly, other cable programs started following the story, as did the broadcast news outlets. For the most part, however, their coverage was as predictable as it was disappointing. Instead of getting into the real stories on the ground, as Schultz and Goodman did, most cable programs devoted inordinate amounts of time to asinine debates between usual-suspect commentators over whether President Obama should "come to Wisconsin" and the extent to which the White House was "orchestrating" the protests. Instead of reporting from Madison, they turned to the same-old talking heads in Washington. It wasn't that networks such as CNN set out to do a bad job. They simply could not figure out how to tell a political story that did not have the president as its punch line.

Of course, some media did set out to do a bad job. When the crowds in Wisconsin grew, when it became clear that the people who were protesting represented a cross-section of middle America, the right-wing echo chamber that repeats corporate and conservative talking points so loudly that they shape the agenda of supposedly "mainstream" media, turned the volume up to 11. The king of conservative radio talkers, Rush Limbaugh, was hysterical, as were most Fox News commentators. They didn't know what to make of a mass movement that wasn't built on the premise that the president was a Kenyan-born Manchurian candidate. Only as the days went on and the crowds in Wisconsin grew did it begin to dawn on them that this genuine grassroots explosion was revealing the Tea Party hype of the previous months for what it is: a faked-frenzy that couldn't mobilize a real crowd to save its own agenda. The confirmation came several weeks into the Wisconsin struggle, when out-of-state operatives sought to organize a "counter protest" in support of the governor. Right-wing talk radio shows talked the event up for days, a fortune was poured into renting buses and ferrying the foot soldiers of the "conservative majority" to the capitol; big-screen monitors were erected, an elaborate stage- and sound-system was put in place, conservative firebrand Andrew Breitbart was flown in. Yet, when the critical Saturday came, the anti-Walker forces outnumbered the pro-Walker crowd by ten to one. Clearly, the right was not going to win the numbers game. It was at this point that Fox flipped over to the fallback position of claiming that the protests were "violent," despite the fact that local police agencies regularly hailed the astonishingly peaceful and gracious nature of the demonstrations. Finally, Wisconsinites started carrying posters that mocked the conservative network with slogans like FOX WILL LIE ABOUT THIS and ACCORDING TO FOX, I'M NOT HERE. The mockery turned to outright laughter when a report on *The O'Reilly Factor* purported to show dangerous demonstrations in Madison; unfortunately, the geniuses at Fox had used old footage of a union dispute in a state with palm trees, which are not common in wintery Wisconsin. Protesters took to carrying inflatable palm trees at the demonstrations, and even began dressing in beachwear, despite the freezing temperatures.

While it was easy to laugh at Fox, it was harder to comprehend the coverage of events in Wisconsin by the *New York Times*. The *Times* can and does produce terrific reporting on a variety of fronts. In many senses, it remains the last bastion of old-school "newspaper of record" seriousness in a media landscape that is littered with the carcasses of once-great newsrooms, thus making it more important—and influential—in today's news landscape than ever before in its history. The *Times* even has something that's lacking at virtually every other print, broadcast, or digital news outlet in America today: a solid labor writer in the person of Steven Greenhouse. Unfortunately, he was not dispatched to Wisconsin to cover the story. The *Times* reporters who did come to Wisconsin brought with them some of major media's worst misconceptions and biases with regard to unions and working-class people. And in so doing they became a part of the story, reinforcing Governor Walker's intransigence.

Walker is a media junkie. He loves politics and voraciously consumes political and government news. He reads newspapers, listens to talk radio, trolls the Internet, and watches cable news shows. And when he is not doing that, he quizzes aides about the latest news. In this sense, the governor of Wisconsin is like a lot of politicians. However, what has always distinguished Walker from many of his peers is his keen interest in the detail and nuance of political coverage. He knows which writers, which publications, which radio shows, and which television networks lean to the left and the right. And so he reads, listens to, and watches media with an eye for how different outlets are interpreting and reacting to stories.

So it was that, when the governor mistakenly took a call from the prankster whom he thought was a Koch brother, the conversation went like this:

WALKER: So it's, uh, this is ground zero, there's no doubt about it. But, uh, I think, you know, for us, I just keep telling, I call, I tell the speaker, the Senate majority leader every night, give me a list of the people I need to call at home, to shore 'em up. The *New York Times*, of all things, I don't normally tell people to read the *New York Times*, but the front page of the *New York Times* has got a great story, one of these unbelievable moments of true journalism, what is supposed to be objective journalism. They got out of the capital and went down one county south of the capital to Janesville, to Rock County, that's where the General Motors plant once was.

"KOCH" CALLER: Right, right.

WALKER: They moved out two years ago. The lead on this story is about a guy who was laid off two years ago, uh, he's been laid off twice by GM, who points out that, uh, everybody else in his town has had to sacrifice except for all these public employees and it's about damn time they do, and he supports me. Um, and they had a bartender, they had, I mean, every stereotypical blue-collar worker type they interviewed, and the only ones that weren't with us were people who were either a public employee or married to a public employee. It's an unbelievable story. So I went through and called all these, uh, a handful, a dozen or so lawmakers I worry about each day and said, "Everyone, we should get that story printed out and send it to anyone giving you grief."

The subject of the February 21 piece was a fellow the *Times* identified as "Rich Hahan [who] worked at the General Motors plant here until it closed about two years ago . . . a union man from a union town."

Unlike the overwhelming majority of Wisconsin union members and former union members—if turnouts at rallies and poll numbers were to be believed—"Hahan" was described as "a supporter of Gov. Scott Walker's sweeping proposal to cut the benefits and collective bargaining rights of public workers in Wisconsin, a plan that has set off a firestorm of debate and protests at the state capitol. He says he still believes in unions but thinks those in the public sector lead to wasteful spending because of what he sees as lavish benefits and endless negotiations."

No surprise that Walker liked the story. And he loved the idea that this was the way elites and people outside of Wisconsin would regard the conflict.

There was only one problem with this scenario.

The *New York Times* got the story wrong. It was bogus. "Hahan" was actually Hahn. And there was no record of the "union man in a union town" ever having been in the Janesville local of the United Auto Workers, which represented employees of the GM plant.

Hence the *New York Times* correction on February 26, which read:

A front-page article on Tuesday about reaction among private sector workers in Wisconsin to Gov. Scott Walker's effort to cut benefits and collective bargaining rights for unionized public employees referred incorrectly to the work history of one person quoted, and also misspelled his surname. While the man, Rich Hahn (not Hahan) described himself to a reporter as a "union guy," he now says that he has worked at unionized factories, but was not himself a union member. (The *Times* contacted Mr. Hahn again to review his background after a United Auto Workers official said the union had no record of his membership.)

The problem, of course, is that the damage was done.

At a critical early point in the debate over whether to strip public employees of their collective bargaining rights, the nation's "newspaper of record" told Scott Walker he was right to presume that "the only ones that weren't with us were people who were either a public employee or married to a public employee." And he diligently peddled that falsehood, in public and private comments, often citing the supposedly liberal and labor-friendly *Times* as his source.

It is rare that we can so precisely pinpoint a moment when media made a difficult situation worse. But this is one of them. Poll after poll after poll showed that the vast majority of Wisconsinites, public sector and private sector, union and non-union, urban and rural, opposed Walker's proposal. The crowds at rallies seeking to kill the bill were the largest in Wisconsin history, and they had drawn workers, farmers, students, and retirees from across the state to Madison and to the town squares of smaller Wisconsin communities from Shullsburg to Sturgeon Bay. Walker should never have been allowed to imagine that there was broad public support for his draconian initiative. Only the *New York Times* permitted him to do so.

The reason the *New York Times* enabled Walker is the same reason that so many major media outlets get so many stories about the organized and unorganized struggles of working Americans wrong. They haven't bothered to cover low-income and working-class Americans seriously for years, choosing instead to tailor their reporting to attract the elite upper-income readers and viewers whom advertisers want to reach. And as reporting staffs have dwindled and bureaus in factory towns have been shuttered so that more attention can be focused on upscale suburbs, the circumstance has grown dramatically worse. One of the best arguments for developing new models for creating and sustaining independent, not-for-profit media is that, by breaking the bondage of upscale demographics and freeing journalists to cover the news, we can get reporters back on the labor beat, back on the streets of working-class communities and back in touch with the reality of struggles such as the one in Wisconsin, rather than the spin that says Americans are just a bunch of greedy bastards who would willingly cut the pay and benefits of their neighbors if there was even the outside chance of a tax break in it for them.

The *Times* actually blew an even bigger piece of the Wisconsin story several weeks later. When Republican legislators used backroom maneuvers to pass Walker's bill, the *Times* reported that the fight was "over."

But the editors in New York forgot to tell the people of Wisconsin.

A day after the *Times* edition of March 11 had reported the end of the struggle, I pulled on a heavy jacket and a good pair of gloves and headed south of Madison to meet up with some farmers. Many of them had done their chores before dawn and then brought their tractors to the edge of their state's capital city.

It was cold and windy. I could barely hear my friend Tony Schultz, a vegetable and beef farmer from Athens in central Wisconsin, and Joel Greeno who had put out the call to members of the Family Farm Defenders and Wisconsin Farmers Union to come to Madison. Finally, Joel shouted, "Let's roll." Fifty tractors fired up and began the three-mile ride into

Madison. Along the side of the road, there were small groups of children with signs reading THANK YOU, FARMERS!

As the tractorcade got closer to town, the crowds grew larger and larger. Passing cars and buses honked their horns. Drivers rolled down their windows and shouted, "Thank you! Thank you!" When the tractors pulled up the hill and onto the great square around the capitol, tens of thousands of Wisconsinites greeted the farmers, with chants of "An injury to one is an injury to all" and "Solidarity!"

Joel Greeno and his fellow farmers had come to say the fight was not over. They were there to join the largest pro-labor mass mobilization in modern American history.

But there was another message that went out that day. The hundreds of thousands of Wisconsinites who rallied at their capitol and in communities across the state said by their very presence that they were no longer going to accept the official "line" from old-media outlets that failed them—and new media outlets that simply compounded the sins of the fathers by aggregating and amplifying the folly of media outlets that have replaced reporting with stenography to power. What dawned on Wisconsinites and their allies in other states was that the problem was not simply the overt bias of a Limbaugh or an O'Reilly but the overt ignorance of media outlets that imagined Americans no longer approved of organized labor— and would never ever stand in solidarity with a trade-union movement that was arguing for public services, public utilities, and public schools.

When media outlets got around to conducting polls on the issues that arose in the Wisconsin struggle, they found that, to paraphrase the old Firesign Theatre routine, everything they "knew" was wrong. A CBS News/*New York Times* survey, conducted shortly after Wisconsin exploded, revealed that six in ten Americans opposed the elimination of collective bargaining rights for public sector union workers, while 56 percent were opposed to the cutting of pay or benefits to reduce state budget deficits. The *USA Today*/Gallup survey released two weeks after Governor Walker made his proposal indicated that 61 percent of Americans were opposed to legislation that would take away the collective bargaining rights of unionized government workers. Only one in three of those surveyed backed any move to undermine protections for labor.

Wisconsin-based blogs, such as Blue Cheddar, recognized the reality on the ground, noting immediately that the crowds at the capitol were packed with farmers, small-business owners, and others who were not union members but who understood the necessity of unions as a counterbalance to corporate overreach. Folks who had never sung "Solidarity Forever" or shouted "An Injury to One Is an Injury to All" knew which side they were on. Because so many Wisconsin-based bloggers did such a fine job of reporting what was happening, it is easy to fall into the trap of thinking that new media got it right while old media got it wrong. But that neglects the fact that Governor Walker's allies were digitally savvy and made ambitious use of the Internet to peddle fantasies about "union thugs" and "out-of-state agitators."

The real story of why Wisconsin exploded—and of why Wisconsin matters for those who consider questions of media and democracy—is not a tale of old media versus new. That tired debate is so 2007.

What emerged in Wisconsin, and what has continued to emerge with the development of the "Occupy Wall Street" and "Occupy Together" movements, is a "Next Media" system, an alternative that is developing right before our eyes. Citizens are creating their own media platforms, combining elements of the oldest and newest media and filling the voids that exist with Facebook pages and Tweets. This Next Media system is more local, more immediate and more diverse that anything that has come before it. This system pushes limits in both directions: new and old. It has room for an old-school morning radio show like that of John "Sly" Sylvester, a former rock-and-roll DJ who made the shift to talk radio a decade ago and established a foothold in Madison with a no-holds-barred approach that was one part Bill Moyers, one part Howard Stern. Raised working-class in Milwaukee, and then Madison, Sly "got" the point of the protests even before they began. On the Monday morning after Walker announced his plan, Sly devoted his entire program, from 6:00 to 10:00 A.M., to featuring the voices of its targets: teachers, snowplow drivers, sanitation workers, and nurses. And he never stopped. Day after day, week after week, month after month, what had been a program that talked about politics became a program where politics played out. Union leaders appeared to announce rallies. Lawyers came on to break down the bills and to explain lawsuits and requests for temporary restraining orders. Legislators called in from the capitol and then, when Democratic senators fled the state to deny Walker's Republicans a quorum, from remote locations in Illinois. Sly took his show to the streets, broadcasting from the middle of demonstrations. Over time, he became one of the steadiest sources of information, and of media criticism, regarding the protests. Many was the day when an absurdly ill-conceived or simply inaccurate report on the front page of the Walker-supporting *Wisconsin State Journal* newspaper had been deconstructed by Sly and his guests before Madisonians had trudged out their front doors to find the offending publication in the snowbank where it had landed.

If Sly realized the full potential of the most democratic of old media constructions—a man with a microphone broadcasting on commercial drive-time media—Madison's community radio station, WORT-FM, and its community television station, WYOU, realized the potential of the "indymedia" experiment that began in Seattle during the 1999 protests against the World Trade Organization. WORT's Norm Stockwell and Molly Stentz made what was already one of the strongest listener-supported stations in the country into a media center, with an open and welcoming studio for independent radio and video producers from across the country. WORT's live broadcasts from marches, rallies, legislative sessions, and courtrooms provided an arc of coverage that was thorough and that captured the news and the excitement of each day—and evening, as WORT's volunteer reporters were often the only broadcast journalists present to witness late-night confrontations.

WORT's work built on the models developed in Seattle, realizing much of the promise of the indymedia movement. No surprise there. Stockwell had been a constant presence domestically and internationally in the development not just of community radio but of independent and alternative media, allied closely with Amy Goodman and indymedia pioneers in the United States and abroad. His presence on the ground in Madison was more than just fortuitous, it was critical to the communications revolution that played out in Wisconsin and beyond.

But that revolution developed on platforms that the indymedia adventurers of Seattle could not have imagined. The 2011 protests in Madison saw a new generation of innovators using the technologies that had revolutionized communications to create a old-and-new media hybrid that provided a rough sense of how radical journalism will be produced and distributed in the future. Notable among the Next Media pioneers of Madison were the editors and reporters from the Center for Media and Democracy (CMD), a local watchdog group that had historically focused its attention on the rigorous analysis of media and public-relations spin. Founded by pioneering media critic and activist John Stauber and currently led by former deputy assistant attorney general Lisa Graves, the center had a popular website and a staff of veteran researchers and young interns. When the Wisconsin protests began, Graves and Mary Bottari made the remarkable decision to create an edited and fact-checked live blog that would cover every aspect of the fight. This unprecedented initiative, rooted in old-media values and indymedia ideals but fully engaging the tools of new media—Facebook, Twitter, texting, flip-cam videos—would in a matter of weeks become so essential that reporters for major newspapers would begin and end their days on CMD's www.prwatch.org site to see what they were missing, to borrow a quote or to check the authoritative schedule of the next day's events in the legislature, in the courts, and on the street.

The CMD folks recognized early on that young videographers such as Madison's Matt Wisniewski were capturing the essence of the moment better than any of the local news reports. Combining still shots, video, and music from Mumford and Sons' "The Cave" and Arcade Fire's "Rebellion (Lies)," Wisniewski's amazing YouTube videos became an Internet phenomenon, attracting millions of viewers first in Madison and Wisconsin but eventually across the country and around the world. By late February, Wisniewski was getting emails from Egyptians telling him that they were following the developments in Wisconsin via his videos. Even *Time* magazine acknowledged that the twenty-three-year-old media specialist with the Great Lakes Bioenergy Research Center "provides us with a view from the capitol that media outlets just can't capture." For Wisniewski, there was an element of pushback, a desire to show a side of the protests that did not come through in drab and dismissive mainstream media reports; "I want to show the true face of what's going on in Madison," he explained, after linking the Mumford and Sons' lyric "but I will hold on hope" with images of protesters returning day after day to the capitol. But he was also creating something fresh, a multimedia mashup of documentary film, *60 Minutes*, and an old-school music video that captured the intensity and the excitement of each day. What had started as an attempt to "show my friends from outside Madison" what was going on became so influential that rocker Tom Morello would incorporate Wisniewski's footage into the popular video of the song he wrote coming off the Wisconsin struggle, "Union Town."

The do-it-yourself character of the Next Media system that developed in Madison was not powered by the old-media stalwarts or independent producers, however. The real heroes were college students, nurses, and teachers Tweeting from the galleries of legislative chambers, from the front rows of courtrooms, from the middle of the crowd when Democratic legislators who had been holed up in Illinois returned to Madison and marched with tens of thousands of Wisconsinites to the steps of the capitol. When the Pew Research Center for the People and the Press studies local media landscapes, it now includes Tweets, and rightly so. The first and freshest reports out of the cacophony that was Madison on the most intense days of the struggle had the immediacy and the intensity that we should expect in our news media; they were ahead of the stories and they got them right, laying the groundwork for the "next roots" to spread. Revolution Messaging's Scott Goodstein, whose own roots are in Wisconsin and who developed some of the first and most effective communications during the struggle, tells the story of a solidarity concert in late February that came together so late in the day that posters could not be printed. A digital version of the poster went out, appearing on phones and computer screens. "Six thousand people showed up," says Goodstein. "We didn't need to kill the trees, we had a better way of getting the message out."

The digital innovators of the Next Media system were high school kids, retirees, and stay-at-home moms who turned their Facebook pages into news sites that grabbed the best of old and new media coverage of what was going on and created a mesh of coverage that connected millions of people from Capitol Square in Madison to Tahrir Square in Cairo with the events that were unfolding in Wisconsin. They sampled old media as ambitiously as a new generation of DJs did the best riffs of sixties rockers or seventies disco artists. When a carefully reported article appeared in the *Nation*, the *Progressive*, the *Milwaukee Journal-Sentinel*, or the *Madison Capital Times*, it was instantly featured on Facebook pages and the feedback was just as instantaneous. I do not use the phrase "Next Media" casually; I have written about media and media systems for the better part of two decades and while I certainly do not claim to know everything about where journalism is headed, I am certain that the organic linkage of a *Nation* story, a podcast from Sly's radio show, a Tweet from a kid sleeping in the capitol, a digital photo album of the best posters from that day's protest, a quote from Howard Zinn, and a clip of Sean Michael Dargan singing "On the Day Scott Walker Is Recalled" was more than mere aggregation, more than blogging. This was a new construct, a Next Media with unprecedented capacity to spread information, to inspire activism, to make real the promise of democracy.

Tech pundits on the left and the right have devoted years to imagining the possibilities of the Internet, straying frequently into a digital utopianism that would have us believe that all the world's problems might be solved with the right click of a mouse. But the predictions have invariably crashed into the reality that new media, while generally easier to produce and distribute than old media, faces the same journalistic challenge confronting quality newspaper and broadcast outlets: resources are scarce and growing scarcer, commercial and entertainment pressures tend to overwhelm civic and democratic values, fickle audiences are so busy exploring where they can "go today" that they do not always stick with and sustain new outlets that need time to find their footing. The template for true twenty-first-century communications has yet to be established, and so the future wrestles with the past. Usually.

There was something about the dynamic of Wisconsin. Perhaps the threat. Perhaps the speed with which the resistance grew. Perhaps the lucky break that so much of the fight played out in Madison, a city with more diverse and independent old media than most and a highly educated, tech-savvy population. Something worked. Old media fed new media, new media informed old, and unprecedented networks of Tweeting teens and Facebooking moms created a journalistic variation on mesh networking that outlined the possibility of a Next Media system. Nothing was finished in Madison or Wisconsin. But something started, and that something was remarkable in scope and character.

It took me time to recognize the full power of what was transpiring. But then, on the first Saturday in March, Michael Moore announced he would be landing in town in a few hours. Because there was no time for traditional organizing or communicating—no time to put posters up or buy ads in newspapers or on radio stations—the CMD folks got the word out on Facebook, along with Susan Stern and members of the Madison Teachers Inc. crisis committee. Local 311 firefighters started texting. Twitter lit up. Folks who were headed for out-state communities to begin passing recall petitions checked their phones and turned back toward Madison. Activists in Milwaukee jumped in their cars. Farmers finished their chores and headed for town. By the time Moore arrived, thousands of teachers and firefighters were assembled outside a downtown fire station. The shocked filmmaker stepped out the front door of the station, took his place behind a unit of bagpipers and drummers, and marched around the city's performing arts center, onto the main street leading toward the capitol, and into a crowd of fifty thousand Wisconsinites. A rally by the grassroots Wisconsin Wave coalition that was going to feature local figures suddenly became a national event, featuring one of the most powerful statements of a burgeoning anti-austerity movement. As Moore spoke, Tweets carried his best lines onto the web. And before his return plane to New York had landed, websites and Facebook pages were featuring Moore's speech, turning a moment in Madison into a global media phenomenon.

The *New York Times,* of course, missed the story, as did the broadcast networks. But they were no longer so necessary as they once had been, and as they might still imagine themselves to be. A Next Media system, forged by old-media renegades, indymedia stalwarts, high school kids and soccer moms in a moment of threat and turmoil, had cracked the communications code, bypassed the gatekeepers, and sent Moore's message straight to the people. A few days later, Michael called me. He had never experienced anything like what happened in Madison, or what happened after he left. Neither had I. We did not try to explain so much as celebrate. We laughed about the folks who were stuck in the ancient debates about old media and new media, who kept trying to keep journalism defined into a box that could no longer contain it. I mentioned something about how it would be hard for people who want simple answers to where journalism and media are headed to embrace the hybrid of old values and new technologies, of Tom Paine and Twitter, that is developing. Michael recalled Bob Dylan's line about a reporter who thought he was hip to the next big thing but kept asking the wrong questions. "Something is happening here / But you don't know what it is / Do you, Mister Jones?" There is something happening. None of us know exactly what it is. The Next Media system has not been fully realized, nor even fully imagined. There is so much yet to be done to develop the models for funding serious journalism in a post-advertising age, to teach new generations of online journalists, to defend the network neutrality that is essential to realize the digital promise, to challenge the prevalence of spin, public relations, and propaganda. But we've got a sense now that a Next Media system is possible; a system that could be more journalistically sound, more democratic, and more radical in its potential than anything we have known since the rise of consolidated and dumbed-down corporate media. We saw glimpses of it in Cairo, then in Madison, then as the "Occupy" movement spread from Wall Street to the world. And those glimpses suggested that the best hope for journalism, and democracy, is a barrier-breaking mashup of old media and new, professional and citizen journalism, innovative cable, indymedia and the grassroots communicators who are turning Twitter and Facebook into something dramatically more important than the digital utopians dared imagine.

The pamphleteer who realized the full potential of the new media of the mid-eighteenth century, using Committees of

Correspondence and circuit riders to forward Tom Paine's "Common Sense" to the revolutionary masses, gave us the language for this moment. "We have it in our power to begin the world over again," Paine wrote. "A situation, similar to the present, hath not happened since the days of Noah until now. The birthday of a new world is at hand."

Paine, the author of a revolution that could not be televised, was referring to a new political order. But his pamphlets confirmed the vital link between journalism and democracy.

If we are to have either, and if we are to take the lesson of why (and how) Wisconsin matters, we would do well to embrace and expand upon the models for a Next Media and a New World that were put on display in 2011 every bit as energetically as Tom Paine did the Next Media and the New World that he recognized in 1776.

CHAPTER 6

The Rise of the House of Labor

Street Heat, Politics as Unusual, and the Evolution of the Mastodon

Ten thousand times has the labor movement stumbled and fallen and bruised itself, and risen again; been seized by the throat and choked and clubbed into insensibility; enjoined by courts, assaulted by thugs, charged by the militia, shot down by regulars, traduced by the press, frowned upon by public opinion, deceived by politicians, threatened by priests, repudiated by renegades, preyed upon by grafters, infested by spies, deserted by cowards, betrayed by traitors, bled by leeches, and sold out by leaders, but notwithstanding all this, and all these, it is today the most vital and potential power this planet has ever known, and its historic mission of emancipating the workers of the world from the thraldom of the ages is as certain of ultimate realization as is the setting of the sun.

—Eugene Victor Debs, 1904

Labor cannot stand still. It must not retreat. It must go on, or go under.

—Harry Bridges, 1937

SCREW US, WE MULTIPLY

—protest sign, Madison, Wisconsin, 2011

L ABOR DID NOT win or lose the Wisconsin struggle. Not yet. And that is a frustrating fact for those who like their uprisings to come neatly packaged and readily analyzed. There is no question that organized labor looked a whole lot healthier than it had for a long time. And it had a lot more friends: farmers, small-business owners, students, retirees, Democrats, and even some Republicans—or, at the least, Wisconsinites who thought they were Republicans right up to the point where they realized that a Republican governor was scheming to kick them out of the middle class.

But was it just an illusion? Was this, as pundits on the right and even sometimes on the left suggested, the last furious struggle before the collapse of a dying behemoth?

I have thought a lot since the onset of the Wisconsin struggle about my friend Tom Geoghegan's brilliant book, *Which Side Are You On? Trying to Be for Labor When It's Flat on Its Back* (FSG, and, more recently, the New Press). Written in 1991, *Which Side Are You On?* touched the hearts and minds of a generation of union members and sympathizers who maintained the faith that A. Philip Randolph, the Brotherhood of Sleeping Car Porters union leader who forged the modern civil rights movement, was right when he said, "The essence of trade unionism is social uplift. The labor movement traditionally has been the haven for the dispossessed, the despised, the neglected, the downtrodden, the poor." We believed passionately in the labor movement, not just for its own purposes but as the underpinning of a broader justice struggle. We knew unions were necessary to everything we hoped and dreamed for our communities, our nation, our world. But we knew, as well, that this made us outliers in a post-industrial, "end of history" moment when "big thinkers" readily entertained the notion that unions were passé. And when the slow decline of the labor movement seemed to suggest that the great mass of Americans shared the assessment. "Organized labor," Geoghegan began. "Say those words, and your heart sinks. I am a labor lawyer, and my heart sinks. Dumb, stupid organized labor: that is my cause. But too old, too arthritic, to be a cause. It was a cause, back in the thirties. Now it is a dumb, stupid mastodon of a thing, crawling off to Bal Harbour to die."

Just reading those words back in 1991 creeped me out. I was a good deal younger than Geoghegan, and a bit more optimistic. I did not want to believe, as a proud member of a union (the Newspaper Guild) and as a writer who still took the role of unions in politics seriously, that labor would not or could not turn itself around. I loved Geoghegan's book, and I hated it. I would go to a World Trade Organization (WTO) protest in Seattle and say, "Well, Tom, you were wrong. Labor's back!" Then I would look at the annual measures of labor union membership and watch them decline, year after year, toward that 10 percent of the workforce line. And I would fear that Tom was right.

But something about the Wisconsin struggle said that, somewhere between faith and realism, somewhere between false hope and bitter acceptance, there might be a way out of the historical abyss. Labor might yet revive and redefine itself as a young, vibrant movement with real strength and a real future. A smart mastodon, if you will, one that amazingly, remarkably, impossibly had survived the Ice Age that swept in when Ronald Reagan busted the Professional Air Traffic Controllers Organization and emerged three decades later not as a fossil but as a fighting force for economic and social justice.

It was hard not to feel hopeful on March 12, the day that 180,000 Wisconsinites welcomed home fourteen Democratic state senators who had fled the state to deny Governor Walker and his Republican legislative allies the quorum required to pass their anti-labor legislation. The Democrats had stayed in Illinois for three weeks, until Republicans broke the legislative logjam by redefining the assault on collective bargaining as a "noneconomic" measure and passing it in the most frenzied moment of official lawlessness since the 2008 federal bank bailout votes that Ohio congresswoman Marcy Kaptur correctly characterized as a financial coup d'état.

Yes, the legislature had acted—in violation of open meetings laws and its own rules—to pass the measure working Wisconsinites had battled for a month to block. But on the Saturday after they did so, the "accomplishment" of Scott Walker and his minions did not look like much of a win.

In fact, it looked as it they had inspired a movement that would reshape politics to the distinct disadvantage of the governor and his party.

When the Democratic senators had decided to exit the capitol and join the movement, rather than simply serve as cogs in the Republican machine, it was one of those rare moments in contemporary political life where labor was calling the shots. Politicians, at least some politicians, were following the lead of the unions and their members, rather than demanding concessions and managing lower expectations.

It seemed on March 12 that anything was possible. Labor was strong. The Democrats were channeling FDR. And the Republicans, instead of celebrating their "victory," were nowhere to be seen. The governor had hightailed it out of Madison, heading six hours north to Washburn, Wisconsin. But even there he could not change the shape of things to come. When Walker arrived at the Washburn supper club where local Republicans were holding a fund-raising event, the place was surrounded by three thousand protesters—in a town of two thousand.

In Madison, there was only one word for what was playing out.

"Wow! shouted state senator Jon Erpenbach, "You go away for a couple of weeks and look at what happens!" Erpenbach, who had gone from relative obscurity to national prominence in the period of three weeks, could not believe his eyes when the former capitol aide surveyed the crowd that had literally surrounded the building to welcome home Wisconsin's dissident senators.

Erpenbach and the other thirteen Democratic senators were greeted as heroes that day. And for good reason. They fled the capitol in mid-February, when Governor Walker and his Republican allies were just hours away from using their legislative majorities to strip state, county, and municipal workers and teachers of their collective bargaining rights. While the Democrats were a distinct minority in the senate, their withdrawal of consent blocked a vote on the legislation for three weeks.

Finally, after the passage of those three weeks, the Republican "nuclear strategy" of tearing apart what had been advanced as a "budget repair bill" and passing its component parts had secured a legislative "win." But the labor movement was celebrating a political victory: the development of a mass movement capable of attracting hundreds of thousands of Wisconsinites to mass rallies in Madison and communities across the state and causing the collapse of Walker's approval ratings even in Republican-sponsored polls.

That movement now proposed to recall at least three Republican state senators who backed the bill, shifting control of the chamber to the Democrats and restoring a system of checks and balances that would end one-party government in Wisconsin. And it prepared for the day when Walker, who under Wisconsin law could not be removed until at least one year after taking office—would himself face a recall. Talk of recalling Walker no longer seemed unreasonable, as poll numbers suggested that the governor was vulnerable to defeat by virtually any Democratic challenger in a new election.

The political dynamics were intense, and even the most optimistic critics of the governor understood that there was much work to do.

But, on that Saturday, everyone was celebrating.

Madison Firefighters Local 311 members marched through the crowd, with pipes and drums blaring. The Reverend Jesse Jackson, actress Susan Sarandon, actor and Wisconsin native Tony Shalhoub joined the line of march as the firefighters wove their way through a crowd that filled the capitol square. Outside a hotel opposite the capitol, the fourteen senators appeared.

The deafening roars of approval shook Madison's downtown before the firefighters—who had rejected the governor's promise of an exemption from the assault on collective-bargaining rights—led the senators through the masses to a stage set up at an entrance to the capitol. A procession that would have taken minutes without the crowd instead took more than an hour, and when the group approached the stage it was almost impossible to move. Finally, they arrived to chants of "Thank you! Thank you!"

The messages from the senators, passionate and pointed, suggested support for the removal of their Republican colleagues and a sense of solidarity with a movement that had made the rights of workers central to a broader campaign for democratic renewal.

"We are going to take our state back. We are going to take our rights back," declared state senator Julie Lassa, a central Wisconsin Democrat who had spent the seventh month of her pregnancy hiding out with fellow senators in neighboring Illinois. She told the crowd, "I have never been prouder to be a Wisconsinite."

That was a common sentiment that Saturday.

There was pride to go around at what would turn out to be the largest political rally ever in Madison—and one of the largest pro-labor rallies in American history.

From the start, the numbers told the story of the labor movement's resistance to Walker's assault on the rights of workers.

The tens.

The hundreds.

The thousands.

The tens of thousands.

The hundreds of thousands.

Wisconsinites from every background, every religion, every politics, and every job had filled the capitol square for the month after the governor announced his scheme.

Their message had been clear and unequivocal. They opposed the assault on working families. They opposed the lawless actions of legislative leaders who were more determined to advance the governor's political agenda than to respect their colleagues or to serve the interests of the state and its citizens.

It had been an exhilarating, frustrating, depressing, and empowering time.

Emotions had soared and collapsed.

But this was a resilient movement. The union members who marched day after frigid day wore pins that celebrated a determination that extended beyond cold and logic. WE FISH THROUGH ICE! read the badges of honor. The protesters told themselves that nothing Scott Walker did to the citizens of the state would be as long lasting or meaningful as what those citizens would do for the state by removing him—and those who had supported him—from office.

Wisconsin's resilience was rooted in its traditions. Wisconsinites learned to work hard in factories and on farms. Most Wisconsinites can trace their roots to a homestead on a country road. Wisconsin is and will always be "America's Dairyland," a farm state with a regard for those who work the land.

So when the farmers had arrived that Saturday, on tractors that rolled in from across the state, Wisconsinites brought the movement full circle. This was a labor movement, to be sure, but not in the narrow sense. This was a labor movement in the broadest sense, taking in every toiling worker.

The tractorcade, organized by the Wisconsin Farmers Union & Family Farm Defenders, began a day of rallying at the capitol that signaled the determination of Wisconsinites to keep fighting the Walker agenda.

"The governor wants to divide us," explained Joel Greeno, as he drove his tractor into the capitol square that morning. "But that won't happen. The governor's got his corporate contributors. But the state employees and the teachers, they've got us. Farmers understand that when you cut funding for road crews and schools, our rural communities get hurt. And we've been hurt enough."

Wisconsin workers and farmers had, in the words of the tractorcade organizers, decided to "Pull Together!" That slogan recalled the historic organizing of the farmer labor movements of the upper Midwest, which had their expression in Wisconsin in the Progressive Party that sent one of "Fighting Bob" La Follette's sons, Robert M. La Follette Jr., to the U.S. Senate, and elected another, Phil La Follette, as governor in the 1930s.

It had been a long time since Wisconsin's working class had seemed so united, and since the farmers and workers of the state had spoken in so loud and clear a voice.

On that Saturday, one of the returning senators put it best. Referring to the decision of the senators to leave for Illinois in order to open up a broader debate, Bob Jauch, a Democrat from far northern Wisconsin, told the crowd, "We did not weaken democracy when we went to the land of Lincoln. We strengthened it."

When Jauch spoke those words, the tens and tens and tens of thousands who had gathered roared their approval, chanting what had become the slogan of a movement: "This is what democracy looks like!"

It was remarkable.

It was epic.

Then, just about everyone went home. And that was where a great debate began.

★ ★ ★

I AM OFTEN asked why organized labor did not call a general strike, pulling out every union member and every worker who could be attracted to the cause. Wisconsin's South Central Labor Federation had embraced the idea and established a council to consider the best tactics for renewing one of the

labor movement's most muscular strategies of old: the mass refusal to work until basic demands were met.

As a young labor reporter, I profiled Harry Bridges, the
longtime leader of the International Longshore and Warehouse
Union, and other leaders of the 1934 San Francisco General
Strike. I had profiled the Flint Sit-Down strikers, whose
takeover of their Michigan factory had played such a critical
role in forging the United Auto Workers union. I knew the
history, and the potential, for mass labor action.

It was that knowledge that made the debate about a general
strike seem a bit odd. Because, of course, there were many days
in February and March of 2011 when what was happening in
Madison met the standard. The state capitol was occupied by
thousands of trade unionists, students, and their allies. Day-
care centers had been set up. Pirate radio stations broadcast
from legislative hearing rooms. Each night, labor films were
shown on the walls of the capitol. Civil rights leaders led the
crowd of occupiers in chants of "We Shall Overcome," nationally prominent singers appeared to give free concerts from
balconies where just a few days earlier lobbyists had plied their
dark arts. On the floor of the rotunda, Miles Kristan and
dozens of other young people maintained an open microphone where workers, students, and musicians had their say
through each day. They were surrounded by drum circles that
maintained a steady rhythm through the day and into the
evening, going silent only as this great mass of humanity settled
in to sleep on marble floors, steps, and benches in a scene that
was at once peaceful and anarchical, serious and good hu-
mored, unprecedented and yet strangely reminiscent of a past
that might have been or a future that might be.

When a student leader chanted "Whose house?" the response came from the far corners of the vast capitol building,

JOHN NICHOLS

a thundering cry of "Our house!" The seat of government was in the hands of the people. And, outside, tens of thousands more people filled the streets for blocks, bringing traffic to a standstill. The police had refused to serve as the governor's "palace guard" and were protecting the right of the unions to assemble and to petition for the redress of grievances. Democratic state senators had fled the capitol to block the process, while Democratic state representatives were holding all-night hearings that kept the building officially open around the clock.

Farmers were riding in from the countryside to show solidarity. Small-business owners were appearing with free coffee and pizzas—thousands of pizzas, paid for by callers from across the country and around the world. Word spread online that Ian's Pizza, which was located a few blocks from the capitol, was delivering to the protesters. Eventually, according to Ian's manager, Staci Fritz, the pizzeria took orders from well-wishers from all fifty states, fifty-eight countries, and Antarctica. The union representing workers on the Suez Canal called, recalls Fritz, who says that "the day we got the call from Egypt—and verified the credit card's address—we realized this had gotten a lot bigger than Italian food."

It was a lot bigger, indeed, than anything the labor movement had seen in decades, perhaps since the 1930s.

What happened in Madison may not have been a general strike in every formal sense. But it was damn near that. And there's nothing wrong with noting the similarities. In fact, there is a good case to be made that labor's mistake was a failure to declare that what was happening was, if not a general strike, then something akin to the radical "Days of Action" that Ontario unions had used so effectively to dramatize their demands in the 1990s.

Could the Wisconsin struggle have been extended to a fuller and more formal general strike? I think so. I understand that many in the labor movement worried at the time, and worry to this day, about whether they had the capacity to play the ultimate card in a labor struggle. Many others worry that tactic might have given Governor Walker an advantage when it came to portraying unions as irresponsible or dangerous. And, certainly, there were questions about when and how government workers can walk off the job, make demands, and realize their goals. None of these debates are wrongheaded; memories of the PATCO (Professional Air Traffic Controllers Organization) fight of 1981 remind us of what happens when some labor leaders count on solidarity and others do not deliver. But the experience of Seattle in 1999, when after several days of hesitancy key unions did show a measure of solidarity with students and environmental activists who had blocked the streets and destabilized the city's downtown, remind us that it is still possible for mass action to turn the course of history. As Public Citizen's Lori Wallach recalls, "The WTO failed to agree on and begin implementing its neoliberal agenda in 1999 because of the protests in Seattle and was thrown off its mission for years afterward."

There are moments when a critical mass has been achieved and a movement has the potential to force the hand of power. My experience as a writer about labor issues and social movements tells me that more could have been done in Madison and Wisconsin on the streets. There were union leaders and political strategists who thought it was essential to turn attention to a state supreme court race pitting a sitting conservative justice with close ties to Walker and an assistant attorney general backed by labor, that would be decided on April 5. Many more were ready to begin the push to recall Republican state senators. The electoral strategies held out the prospect of using the energy of the street protests to achieve change at the polls: flipping control of the supreme court so that a pro-labor majority was in charge, shifting the center of gravity in the senate so that the governor's legislative agenda would be stymied. As it happens, the electoral approach brought mixed results: a narrow and controversial defeat in the April 5 court race, the defeat of two Republican state senators on August 9 but not the three required to shift control. There are critics who see in these results confirmation that electoral strategies are doomed. I disagree. But electoral politics cannot be the sole political focus of labor. Rather, the combination of street heat and electoral action, though difficult to achieve, seems to make the most sense. The two can and should go hand in hand; in fact, I think the combination of the two is far more powerful than the sum of the parts.

But will labor "get" the calculus right?

Perhaps. And if it does happen, there can be no doubt that the roots of labor's renewal were planted in Wisconsin.

That's because savvy union leaders did not just come to Madison to speak and march. They came to look and listen.

Mary Kay Henry spent a day in late February talking with many of the thousands of Wisconsinites who had packed the state capitol for the protests against Walker's proposals to scrap collective bargaining rights and slash funding for public education and services. As she waited in a legislative hearing room that had been turned into a makeshift studio for a Pennsylvania labor radio show, the new president of the 2.2-million–member Service Employees International Union (SEIU) was marveling at what she had seen. "It's inspiring, so inspiring, but we have to pay attention to what's happening here," she said, in a calm, thoughtful voice. "We've got to take this national, and we've got to keep the spirit, the energy. We've got to do it right."

Henry was not just speaking in the excitement of the moment. Even before the Wisconsin uprising and ensuing demonstrations in Ohio, Indiana, Michigan, and Maine, SEIU had been drawing the outlines of a "Fight for a Fair Economy" campaign that would use the resources of the union to mobilize low-wage workers—be they union members or not—into a movement aimed at transforming a national debate that for too long has been warped by conservative talking points about the need for an "America is broke" austerity and ginned-up Tea Party "populism." After the frustrating experience of trying to get the Employee Free Choice Act through a supposedly friendly Congress in the first two years of President Obama's administration, Henry and a growing number of labor leaders are coming to recognize that simply electing Democrats is not enough. A memo that circulated in January 2011, among members of the union's executive board declared, "We can't spark an organizing surge without changing the environment, so that workers see unions not as self-interested institutions but as vehicles through which they can collectively stand up for a more fair economy."

In the immediate aftermath of the mobilizations in Madison and other state capitals, there was a tentative but emerging consensus that mass movements at the state level might matter just as much to the broader goals of labor and the left as traditional election-oriented campaigning. As Steve Cobble, former political director of the Reverend Jesse Jackson's "Rainbow Coalition" project, explained it, "The energy that's developed in Wisconsin and Ohio, and that could develop in a lot of other states, is what's needed to renew the coalitions that can re-elect President Obama in 2012 and elect a lot of

Democrats. But it should go further than that. With the right organizing push, unions can build a base that forces Obama and the Democrats to take more progressive stands and to govern accordingly."

The size of the demonstrations in the states, and the agility with which protest movements pivoted to political fights that had the potential to shift control of governorships and legislatures, prompted a reassessment of strategy by labor and its allies. Rather than a single-minded focus on electing Democrats, the rare friendly Republican or a third-party ally, there was at least some entertainment of the notion, a basic tenet of radical union activists for a generation, that more will be accomplished by directing cash and organizing hours to (as one SEIU draft document suggested) "mobilizing underpaid, underemployed, and unemployed workers" and "channeling anger about jobs into action for positive change."

Not everyone, even within the progressive labor world, had full confidence in this approach. Activists and analysts I respect, people like labor writer Steve Early, have argued from frustrating experience that too many major unions seem to be incapable of breaking out of a dysfunctional relationship with the Democratic Party, a relationship that again and again has seen organized labor dial down militancy in order to serve the immediate electoral demands of a party that never really delivers for labor when it's in power.

Early is not a cynic. He recognizes, as we all must, that changing the way that labor does politics is always easier said than done.

Even as she explored the option of a different approach, SEIU's Henry conceded that the decision to focus more on nonunion workers was risky. After all, what was being proposed was a major expenditure of resources, with some fifteen hundred SEIU staffers fanning out in seventeen cities to knock on more than three million doors—including those of millions of non-SEIU members.

There are real debates, legitimate debates, to be had about labor's commitment and capacity. They have been inspired, energized, and influenced by what played out in Wisconsin. But they are not going to end because of what has happened, because of what may happen in any one state, or even what might happen as a result of movements such as Occupy Wall Street. That's not something we should bemoan. In *Which Side Are You On?* Tom Geoghegan wrote: "I try to think of the AFL-CIO in the year 2001. But I cannot do it. The whole idea is too perverse."

Yet, two decades after Geoghegan was writing, and a decade after it was "too perverse" to imagine where labor might stand, the movement is actually debating tactics and strategies. That's more than a sign of life. That's the outlining of a future. And what's encouraging is that some of those tactics and strategies address the very challenges that so concerned Geoghegan in 1991.

Despite differences over precise approaches, there was in 2011 a growing understanding that the greatest threats to unions as forces in the workplace and in political life were developing at the state level, where GOP governors and legislators are attacking collective bargaining rights while proposing brutal cuts in spending on education and services, and where the cuts sought by some Democratic governors are only slightly less painful. These are not isolated threats, they are coordinated projects of corporate interests, using vehicles such as the American Legislative Exchange Council (ALEC).

Founded in 1973 by Paul Weyrich and other conservatives who wanted to place a one-size-fits-all imprint on state policies,

ALEC has become a critical arm of the right-wing network of policy shops and advocacy organizations that, with infusions of corporate cash, has evolved to shape American politics. Inspired by Milton Friedman's call for conservatives to "develop alternatives to existing policies [and] keep them alive and available," ALEC's model legislation reflects long-term goals: downsizing government, removing regulations on corporations, and making it harder to hold the economically and politically powerful to account. Corporate donors retain veto power over the language, which is developed by the secretive task forces made up of corporate insiders and conservative legislators.

ALEC did, indeed, place a conservative imprint on the states in 2011, when the group included bills to privatize education, break unions, deregulate major industries, pass voter ID laws, and eliminate whatever restrictions remained on corporate campaign spending. Stacks of new laws that got their start with ALEC were signed by GOP governors like Wisconsin's Scott Walker and Ohio's John Kasich, both ALEC alums. But ALEC pushed too hard and too far in 2011, leading an insider to leak the model bills that had previously been available only to the group's two thousand legislative and three hundred corporate members. With the aid of Aliya Rahman, an Ohio-based activist who helped organize protests at ALEC's Spring Task Force meeting in Cincinnati, the Center for Media and Democracy and the *Nation* obtained more than eight hundred documents representing decades of model legislation and exposed ALEC's manipulations on behalf of a list of billionaire benefactors that included Tea Party funders Charles and David Koch.

Common Cause's Bob Edgar said that the documents and details revealed by the ALEC Exposed project confirmed that "dozens of corporations are investing millions of dollars a year to write business-friendly legislation that is being made into law in statehouses coast to coast, with no regard for the public interest. This is proof positive of the depth and scope of the corporate reach into our democratic processes." And, above all, they showed that disempowering and diminishing the power of labor unions was job one for some of the most powerful corporate and political interests in the United States.

In the face of genuine threats to their own existence and to the democratic discourse that they make real by providing at least some counterbalance to corporate power, savvy leaders of the unions that hoped to survive recognized that they had to adopt more flexible, independent, and aggressive approaches.

SEIU and other national labor and progressive organizations were not rejecting all the old ways. Unions were still going to expend resources to elect political friends and defeat political enemies, hedging union bets at a point when fears about the impact of the Supreme Court's *Citizens United* ruling have created dramatic, and frequently unreasonable, pressures to match the spending of Republican-aligned forces. But after too many years of steering enormous energy into national election campaigns—only to be confronted with presidential caution, congressional gridlock, and the rise of an extreme and energized Republican right—savvy union leaders such as Henry, NNU's DeMoro, and Randi Weingarten of the American Federation of Teachers were frankly acknowledging that they must be more than mere cogs in party machines.

"We are looking hard at how we work in the nation's political arena. We have listened hard, and what workers want is an independent labor movement that builds the power of working people—in the workplace and in political life," AFL-CIO president Richard Trumka explained in a May 2011 National Press Club address. "Our role is not to build the power of a political party or a candidate. It is to improve the lives of working families and strengthen our country."

Trumka was not saying that labor unions would no longer back the Democratic party and Democratic candidates, up to and including a disappointing but sympathetic president like Barack Obama. There's little doubt that labor will continue to lean toward the party of Franklin Roosevelt and Harry Truman. What Trumka was saying, however, is that labor will not simply back Democrats because they are Democrats.

"We'll be less inclined to support people in the future that aren't standing up and actually supporting job creation and the type of things that we're talking about. It doesn't matter what party they come from. It will be a measuring stick," explained Trumka, a frequent visitor to Wisconsin and other states during the labor rights battles of 2011.

The Press Club address, a high-profile initiative by the leading figure in the American labor movement, included a warning to Democratic officials who think they can make draconian cuts in education and public service—or that they can undermine union rights—simply by claiming that the Republicans would make crueler cuts.

"It doesn't matter if candidates and parties are controlling the wrecking ball or simply standing aside—the outcome is the same either way," said Trumka, acknowledging the bipartisan character of the austerity lie. "If leaders aren't blocking the wrecking ball and advancing working families' interests, working people will not support them. This is where our focus will be—now, in 2012 and beyond."

Practically, what Trumka was talking about was replacing the traditional pre-election mobilization of the union faithful with year-round organizing that is more oriented toward issues and immediate struggles.

But, as is always the case with Trumka when the AFL-CIO president is at his best, there was an idealistic component to the initiative.

At the root of Trumka's message was an idea that needs to be returned to the center of the political discourse.

"America's real deficit is a moral deficit—where political choices come down to forcing foster children to wear hand-me-downs while cutting taxes for profitable corporations," said Trumka, recognizing that the current assault on labor rights is about more than contracts and collective bargaining. It is designed to prevent unions from raising moral concerns in the midst of budget debates.

"Powerful political forces are seeking to silence working people—to drive us out of the national conversation," explained the AFL-CIO president, who noted the irony of anti-labor Republicans hailing the Reverend Martin Luther King Jr. while neglecting to recall that King died while in Memphis to rally support for striking sanitation workers. "I can think," Trumka said, "of no greater proof of the moral decay in our public life than that Wisconsin governor Scott Walker would dare give a Martin Luther King Day speech hailing Dr. King at the same time that he drafted a bill to take away collective bargaining rights from sanitation workers in Wisconsin."

If organized labor seeks to add a moral component to the debate, and if it uses its still-considerable political muscle to back those Democrats, Greens, independents, and, yes, Republicans who are willing to embrace a more class-conscious politics, it could become as influential a player in coming election cycles as the Tea Party movement was in 2010.

To do this, however, Trumka and his allies must meet two requirements that will demand not just new thinking but new commitments on the part of the labor movement:

1. **Labor has to go grassroots,** by supporting the union, farm, student, and community coalitions that are resisting cuts in states across the country and that are fighting any attempt to undermine Medicare, Medicaid, and Social Security by politicians of both parties in Washington. Building and strengthening these coalitions in states such as Wisconsin, Florida, Indiana, Maine, Michigan, Ohio, and Pennsylvania—all of which happen to be presidential battleground states—is the single best investment in progressive, pro-labor politics heading into the 2012 cycle. It creates an infrastructure that is not just about winning one election for one candidate or party but that seeks to achieve practical ends, both immediately and in the long term.

2. **Labor must be ready to put real pressure on the Democrats,** by supporting smart primary challenges (as they did to some extent in 2010) and by withholding money from incumbents who have let them down. Labor must look for Republicans who are willing to break with their party on key issues—something that the union movement historically did with such success that, into the 1990s, there were Republican legislators in states across the country (and a few members of the U.S. House and Senate) who maintained strong pro-labor voting records. And labor must recognize the value of independent and third-party campaigns that, with sufficient union backing in communities where an independent labor-left infrastructure has been or might be established (San Francisco, Los Angeles, Seattle, Portland, Boulder, Missoula, Minneapolis and St. Paul, Madison, Detroit, Toledo, Burlington, Boston, to name but a few), could elect pro-union stalwarts and put real pressure on both major parties.

Ultimately, party labels mean very little. It's the policies that matter. And to the extent that the labor movement recognizes this fundamental political reality, we will have a better politics in Wisconsin, in Ohio, in Maine, and across the United States.

This all sounds so logical on paper.

But labor isn't always logical.

The details of what Trumka describes as a "full-time, around-the-calendar political program," as opposed to a purely election-focused plan, were still being hashed out by the federation as the 2012 election approached. Different unions were developing distinct approaches. But one thing was clear: real change won't be implemented through the centralized, one-size-fits-all processes many Beltway-based groups are used to. "Of course, it's easier to come up with some big national plan and say everyone's got to buy in," explained Michael Lighty, director of public policy for the California Nurses Association/National Nurses United. "When you are working in the states, you have to be a lot more attuned to the grassroots, and to the distinct politics of communities."

States have unique political cultures, quirky voting patterns, divides between heavily union and nonunion regions that can be finessed only by those who understand the territory. "I've heard from people in other states who want to know how they can do what's been done in Wisconsin, and I tell them it's not that easy," says Ben Manski, an organizer of the Wisconsin Wave protest coalition. "They have to focus in on their own strengths, their own history and their own challenges."

Wisconsin activists focused in 2011 on recall elections that would remove two Republican state senators who had backed Walker's anti-labor agenda, and in 2012 on recalling Walker. Mainers were lobbying moderate Republican legislators to break with right-wing governor Paul LePage. While there was talk in Michigan of trying to recall Governor Rick Snyder, in Ohio there was no recall option. So in Ohio attention turned to a veto referendum provision that unions used to overturn Governor John Kasich's attacks on collective bargaining.

Every one of these state battles turned a labor struggle that initially played out in the streets into an edgy political fight. Instead of waiting for the next election, labor and progressive campaigners were forcing votes on their schedules to address unprecedented assaults on union rights and public services.

Electoral struggles rarely produce definitive results. And that was the case in Wisconsin with the summer 2011 recall races. A total of nine recall votes was held over the course of five weeks in July and August of 2011. Six involved Republican incumbents targeted by Democrats. Three involved Democratic incumbents targeted by Republicans. Opponents of Governor Walker's attacks on collective-bargaining rights prevailed in the majority of recall elections and claimed the majority of votes cast in what many saw as a statewide referendum on Walker's policies. Two Republican senators were defeated, while all the Democrats won by comfortable margins.

That meant that Democrats narrowed the Republican advantage in the Wisconsin senate to from a daunting 19–14 divide to a narrow 17–16 split, which put a moderate Republican senator who opposed Walker's assault on collective-bargaining rights in a position to work with Democrats to temper the extremes of the governor and his allies.

Republicans were quick, and within their rights, to point out that the Democrats did not succeed in taking control of the state senate, an ardent hope of the opposition party and its allies as they pursued their efforts to oust GOP senators in Republican districts across the state.

But the final tallies from a summer of recall elections confirmed that the governor and his supporters had suffered not just defeats in districts located in the north, south, east, and west of the state but also a serious blow to their authority inside the state capitol.

"Scott Walker's working majority in the Wisconsin state Senate is over," announced the labor-backed group We Are Wisconsin after the last of the recall votes, which produced two big wins for the Democrats, were declared. "[The] chamber now boasts a pro-worker majority that would not have passed the budget repair bill that touched off this entire fight."

That was not hyperbole. The sixteen senate Democrats—fourteen who went to Illinois in February and March to block legislative action on the governor's proposal and two new members who beat Republican incumbents who sided with the governor—all were defenders of collective-bargaining rights. Add to that total moderate Republican senator Dale Schultz, who broke with his caucus to oppose the budget repair bill, and it was indeed the case that the senate majority has shifted against the governor on the issue that provoked both the mass street demonstrations against the governor's agenda and the recalls.

The last of the summer's recall elections took place six months after Governor Walker proposed his plan to strip away collective-bargaining protections that had been enjoyed for five decades by state, county, and municipal employees and teachers, and five months after the governor's legislative allies passed the measure without any Democratic votes.

The bitter debate surrounding those moves provoked the rush to recall state senators and set up an epic battle that pitted labor against corporate power on a complex electoral playing field.

National conservative groups and their Republican allies announced early on that they would go after the Democratic senators who had left the state to try to block Walker's plan.

Unions and their Democratic allies then moved to recall Republican senators who had sided with Walker.

With the August 19 wins for the Democrats, the most closely watched series of special elections in American history—and, with $43 million in spending, one of the most expensive political fights the country had ever seen—was finished.

Even as Republicans and their corporate allies tried to spin the fantasy that anything less than complete victory for labor and the Democrats was a defeat, the results renewed talk of recalling Walker. By mid-November 2011, more than 200,000 Wisconsinites had pledged to work for the removal of the governor; and the recall drive was on. It was not just wishful thinking to believe that the governor could be removed; indeed, polls confirmed that his approval ratings had tanked over the course of 2011. And guerrilla politics, which forced elections on labor's schedule rather than that of the political insiders, had shifted the dynamic from 2010, when the Republicans had the advantage. On the night of the last of Wisconsin's state senate recalls, Michael Sargeant, the executive director of the national Democratic Legislative Campaign Committee, celebrated a "broad rebuke of the Wisconsin GOP's out-of-touch, anti–middle class agenda" and heard "a warning shot in the ongoing fight against right-wing extremism in states across the country."

No one knows exactly how the fight will play out. Walker and other Republican governors will face recalls, referendums, and revolts. In Ohio, where labor led and Democrats followed, the results were spectacular—a 61–39 landslide for labor rights in the November 2011, referendum vote. But there are no guarantees that state-based initiatives will always be so well-focused and successful.

There will be resistance to the more aggressive and, arguably, dangerous politics of an independent and unapologetic labor movement. Indeed, there already has been. The Wisconsin senate recall drive pulled punches. National consultants sought to soften the message of Democratic challengers to Republican senators. Wisconsin Democratic Party officials actually suggested at one point that the recalls were not about collective bargaining. Instead of mounting a coordinated statewide campaign that capitalized on the energy and passion of the previous winter's protests, the summer's recall races were cautious affairs that tended too frequently to mirror traditional campaigns: with negative television ads, the politics of personality and local themes trumping the big-picture messages that might have fully realized the potential to make the recalls a referendum on Walker, the assault on labor, and corporate-power false premises of the Republican push for austerity.

Practitioners of the old politics will tell you that it is hard to say what might have happened if the campaigns in Wisconsin had taken a more militant turn. I disagree. My sense from covering campaigns in all fifty states, but especially in Wisconsin, is that soft messaging creates an opening for political consultants—with virtually unlimited funding from national interests—to use negative advertising to depress and suppress voter turnout. My sentiments have always been with Vermont senator Bernie Sanders, who as an independent socialist has argued across three decades of successful campaigning in a historically Republican state that labor and the left do best when they present a clear alternative to the right.

That said, even the mild campaigns that played out in Wisconsin during the summer of 2011 were too much for some Democratic consultants and labor strategists. How so?

What happened in Wisconsin and what may yet happen there, what played out in Ohio and may yet play out in Michigan and other states, was not politics as usual. It scared some

Democrats, especially D.C. insiders who didn't want to be pulled in fifty different directions. They worried that these new efforts would draw attention and resources away from the party's 2012 game plan.

But an independent labor movement is not necessarily bad news if national Democrats are willing to adapt in the same way that Ohio Democrats did, and that the wisest Wisconsin Democrats have.

President Obama and the political operations associated with him, including the Democratic National Committee and Organizing for America, maintained an arm's-length stance during the epic state-based labor struggles of 2011, offering some supportive words but not a lot of physical presence where unions were fighting Republican governors. Obama, a regular presence in Wisconsin in 2009 and 2010, did not visit the state during the course of the protests or the state senate recall fights.

The truth about Obama in 2011 was that he and his political aides were hoping to stand above the turbulence in the states, while still reaping benefits from it. Even as the president carefully avoided getting in the thick of the fight over Walker's proposal, Obama's approval ratings edged up in a state where the polarization between Republicans and Democrats had become stark. That's a dynamic the White House recognized. "The president's political people . . . watch what's happening in the battleground states," Steve Cobble, who has engaged in presidential politics since 1972, explained in the fall of 2011. "So if these movements start to pick up steam, if the unions start getting things going, that's the best way to get the notice of Democrats in Washington and to get them to say and do more on the economic justice issues."

Even as the White House was watching and waiting, some senior Democrats "got" the significance of what was happening in the battleground states, and their experience was instructive. Ohio senator Sherrod Brown, a freshman Democrat up for re-election in 2012 in a state that backed Obama in 2008 but then swung hard to the Republicans in 2010, argued throughout 2011 that Governor John Kasich's "outrageous" assault on collective bargaining provided an opening for a bolder politics. Brown threw himself into the Ohio fight on labor's behalf, using personal appearances, media interviews, and his website to urge on protests and gather support for the fight to overturn anti-labor legislation with the veto referendum. "Ohio Republicans are waging a full scale war on working families," declared Brown. His words and deeds were far more aggressive than D.C.-based consultants ever recommend for senators facing tough reelection races. But polls conducted after Brown started speaking out found him opening up a wide lead over prospective Republican challengers. "Sherrod Brown appears to be in a much stronger position now than he was just three months ago," explained Public Policy Polling president Dean Debnam late in the spring of 2011. "There's been a very significant shift in the Ohio political landscape toward the Democrats."

In many senses, Brown's approach represented a dream scenario for progressives in the labor movement. Republicans push too hard; labor pushes back and elects Democrats aligned with the unions, strengthening both the labor movement and the party's electoral prospects. But Brown has always been a more labor-friendly and adventurous Democrat than most. The challenge is to build state-based movements that are muscular enough to win immediate fights (blocking bad legislation, preventing cuts, preserving embattled unions, organizing new workers) while pulling Democrats—from the local level to the White House—away from the politics of caution and compromise.

The Fight for a Fair Economy program that the SEIU outlined after the Wisconsin fight blew up reflected this sort of
long-term thinking, with its emphasis on using door-to-door
community organizing to reach out to union members and
nonmembers and build mass movements of low-income and
working-class people in Cleveland, Detroit, Miami, Milwaukee, and other cities. Instead of merely steering tens of millions
of dollars from the union treasury into traditional political organizing, with a tight emphasis on gearing up for elections,
SEIU's plan envisioned mobilizing coalitions to fight at the
state level for public services and public education, to mount
mass protests like those seen in Wisconsin, and to engage in
local and state policy fights. Electing better policymakers is
part of the equation, but the emphasis on neighborhood organizing, coalition building, and demonstrations suggests that
what is created could have significantly more staying power
than campaigning as usual.

SEIU's was not the only initiative by a major union that
proposed to take it to the states in the aftermath of the Wisconsin uprising. Communications Workers of America (CWA)
president Larry Cohen responded to attacks on collective bargaining by promoting a "We Are One" campaign that attracted
broad support and helped produce hundreds of April 4, 2011,
rallies and teach-ins to oppose the assault on workers' rights.
National Nurses United (NNU) went into the thick of the
Wisconsin protests with its "Blame Wall Street" campaign,
which called for addressing "the budget deficit with a just re-
balancing of the responsibility of the corporate elite and the
rich." That message, which went national later in 2011 via
NNU's "Contract with Main Street" campaign, remains vital
to shifting a debate that too frequently begins with an assumption that officials have no option aside from cuts. And it is being

amplified by groups such as National People's Action, which are ramping up their own "Make Wall Street Pay" campaigns against big banks (including Wells Fargo, JPMorgan Chase, and Bank of America). These campaigns focus on foreclosure fights and going on the offense to fix the revenue crisis. Even as the Wisconsin protests were playing out, the new US Uncut movement was invading bank lobbies and corporate headquarters with the message "No Cuts Until Corporate Tax Cheats Pay Up!" Later in the spring, groups like Americans United for Change, MoveOn.org, and Progressive Democrats of America were cheering on the heated challenges to proposed Medicare and Medicaid cuts that so rattled congressional Republicans like House Budget Committee chairman Paul Ryan, R-Wisconsin, at town hall meetings that were every bit as raucous as those the Tea Party visited in 2009 and 2010. And the fall 2011 Occupy Wall Street project, which quickly evolved into an Occupy Together movement targeting cities across the country, took the politics of protest to new levels of intensity and messaging.

The tactical shift toward mass mobilization and action—as opposed to relying merely on election-focused list building, member education, and media campaigns—has been casually compared to the ginning up of the Tea Party movement by billionaires David and Charles Koch and their allies after the battering Republicans took in the 2008 elections. To the extent that these new initiatives emphasize mass rallies and a presence at town meetings held by Ryan and other Republican Congress members, the comparison is appropriate. The difference, of course, is that unions are genuinely popular organizations, unlike Koch Industries. The relationship of these efforts to the Democratic Party, moreover, is not so straightforward as that of the Kochs, the Tea Party, and the GOP.

In fact, the relationship between labor and the Democratic Party is in many senses more distant than at any time since the 1920s.

On April 4, 2011—the very day "We Are One" rallies urged on by CWA's Cohen and allies were taking place across the country—President Obama signaled that he was taking the first step toward formalizing his reelection campaign. Obama and his crew could not have been unaware of the We Are One mobilization, but they did not so much embrace it as surf it. If that remains the pattern for high-level Democrats, it is hard to see how state-based organizing will "change the environment" sufficiently to produce a national electoral politics that is about creating a fair economy—as opposed to kinder, gentler variations of GOP budget-tightening proposals. It was clear as the 2012 election season approached that, if the efforts to mobilize new coalitions in 2011 simply evolved into traditional union election work in 2012, that could help Obama. But it was hard to see how that would spawn a more labor-friendly politics.

An awareness of this led one union with a history of providing potent support to national Democrats to announce in April 2011 that it would shift its focus to state and local fights. Expressing deep frustration with the failure of national Democrats to advance pro-labor federal legislation or to aggressively back union battles in the states, the International Association of Fire Fighters (IAFF) announced it would indefinitely suspend all contributions to federal candidates. "It's a pattern of disappointments. . . . Our friends simply have not found a way to actually deliver on behalf of workers and the middle class," explained IAFF president Harold Schaitberger, whose members—often in uniform—had been out front at state and local demonstrations to preserve collective bargaining rights and oppose service cuts. "We are . . . turning the spigot

off and we are redirecting our resources and our efforts out to
the various states where we are fighting these fights." To have
the greatest impact, though, the focus on state-level work must
involve more than shifting money from federal to state campaign treasuries. Real movements must be built in the states
to hold officials to account and keep low-income and working-class Americans engaged as they push ideas up from the
local and state levels to the federal level.

Labor leaders with any sense of the current crisis are con-
scious of these demands, but they would do well to consider
a historical precedent. After the 1932 election, Franklin Roosevelt found himself possessed of the presidency and Democratic majorities in the House and Senate. But he did not have
the kind of majorities he needed to advance all of what came
to be known as the New Deal. One of his great challenges
was that in key states—California, Washington, North Dakota,
Minnesota, Wisconsin, and New York, among others—labor
and farm groups were developing left-leaning movements that
often operated beyond the boundaries of the Democratic
Party. *Time* magazine referred to a moment when "the U.S.
political ferment" was beginning to "seethe, burble, and spill
over in dozens of different places."

As the 1934 and 1936 elections approached, Roosevelt recognized that he had to align with these groups, even if it put
him at odds with some conservative Democrats, to build the
broad coalition he needed. In the summer of 1934, after a wave
of militant labor organizing and localized general strikes had
swept cities across the country, Roosevelt came to Wisconsin,
where Senator Robert La Follette Jr. and former governor
Philip La Follette were forging an independent Progressive
Party. Knowing that he could not dance around the question
of his relationship with the Wisconsin Progressives, the Min-

nesota Farmer-Laborites, and groups like them across the country, the president distanced himself from the conservatives in his own party, hailed the La Follettes, and delivered a populist appeal for unity "irrespective of many older political traditions" to battle the economic royalists who would turn the country back toward "the old law of the tooth and the claw."

Responding to the state-based movements of his day, Roosevelt proposed a dramatically more ambitious politics that "recognizes that man is indeed his brother's keeper, insists that the laborer is worthy of his hire, demands that justice shall rule the mighty as well as the weak."

The appeal worked, as left-leaning movements in the states organized independently on behalf of Roosevelt's program. That expanded the New Deal coalition, giving Democrats and independent progressives historic victories and preparing the ground for FDR's landslide 1936 reelection. Times have changed. There's no confusing a Barack Obama with Franklin Roosevelt. But those who would dare to dream that the Democrats might yet be turned toward a more aggressively progressive and militantly pro-labor politics would be wise to note the lesson of history and of Wisconsin. Organized labor can and must recognize that the hard work of building independent movements in the states remains the best route to changing the politics of the nation.

I know that's a tall order.

I also know that Tom Geoghegan proposed pretty much the same thing twenty years ago.

But 1991 was a long time ago and far away.

It was before Clinton and Bush (well, the second Bush). Before Barack Obama went into politics, and before Fox News went on air. Before NAFTA and GATT and the WTO and Seattle. Before deindustrialization hit its stride, before we knew we were living in a bubble economy, before mortgage meltdowns, bank bailouts or *Capitalism: A Love Story.* Before the spin doctors came up with the lie that the wealthiest nation in the world was broke and Glenn Beck figured out how to make at least some working people believe it. Before anyone in their right mind, or anyone in their wrong mind for that matter, thought it was politically safe to propose privatization of Social Security, voucherization of Medicare, or the end of public education as we know it. Before the *Citizens United* ruling or the realization that, with corporations unbound by campaign-finance limits, even our democracy is up for bid. Before the Tea Party and Scott Walker and the win-at-any-cost politics that says an election victory is not just an excuse to govern, it's an excuse to crush your opponents into oblivion. And before we knew that Americans who had been pushed and pushed and pushed would finally leave their homes and workplaces, go to the streets and push back.

Before Wisconsin.

When Tom Geoghegan was describing organized labor as a mastodon crawling off to die, he was sad and sorry. And rightly so. But the mastodon did not die. It got weak, tragic even, but it blustered on. Then a funny thing happened in 2011. A whole lot of people, thousands of people, tens of thousands of people, hundreds of thousands of people, millions of people, realized that they needed the mastodon. The mastodon started to evolve. And it was no longer perverse to imagine organized labor as an essential force in the economic and political life of the republic. It was necessary, and something else: exciting.

Afterword

The Remedy Is to Begin Anew

> The governing rule of right and mutual good must in
> all public cases prevail.
>
> —Thomas Paine, "Public Good," 1780

THE WISCONSIN UPRISING was and is just that: an uprising. Like every uprising from which it took inspiration,
from Seattle to the Spring 2006 immigrant rights mobilization
to the "Arab Spring" that spread from Tunis to Cairo and beyond, and like every uprising it inspired, from Indianapolis to
Columbus to Wall Street, it always was and always will be
about more than one moment, more than one place, more
than one fight. Tom Paine, who gave us the language of revolt
and revolution, also gave us the language for understanding
uprisings not as solitary events but as arcs that extend from be-
ginnings we barely recognize to ends we cannot quite make
out. "Man advances from idea to idea, from thought to
thought," wrote Paine in 1791, "and all the time he is unaware
of his marvelous progress."

What happened in Wisconsin in February and March of
2011 was a marvelous progress. Michael Moore recognized it as
the response that should have come to the financial meltdown

of 2008. But it was more even than that. It was the pushback against three decades of crackpot economics, the recognition that Ronald Reagan's fantasy that wealth redistributed upward to an elite one percent would somehow serve the other 99 percent had finally and formally been disproven. Trickle-down economics had failed, miserably. It might once have been a live prospect intellectually, but it was now just a zombie idea, lurching toward what was left of the American dream. And the working people of Wisconsin were not inclined to be victims in the horror film sequel that the Koch brothers and ALEC and Scott Walker were scripting.

But an awakening does not always, in and of itself, provide deliverance. Money and power were not about to surrender the trickle-down fantasy that had served their purposes so well across the 1980s, the 1990s, and the 2000s. Even as Governor Walker's personal approval ratings tanked during the course of 2011, even as his legislative allies faced recall and removal from office, even as Walker himself was targeted for electoral ejection, the governor and his minions kept peddling the zombie idea, hoping that they could strangle the uprising in Wisconsin—or, at the least, keep it from spreading.

★ ★ ★

THAT'S WHERE Sarah Palin came in.

In mid-April of 2011, Walker's allies decided to make their stand on the square surrounding the capitol in Madison. They would prove, they promised, that there was a silent majority of Wisconsinites who despised public employees, who wanted less government and more privatization, who dreamed of paving the commons and parking their BMWs on it. The governor was in full spin mode. Though implementation of his anti-union agenda had been stymied by a court order, the gov-

ernor flew to Washington for a star turn before a congressional committee where his fellow Republicans made every effort to suggest that he had effectively overwhelmed the mass opposition that his proposals had inspired. It was announced on right-wing talk radio that on the following Saturday, April 16, Palin would jet into Madison for what was supposed to be a victory party.

All that was needed was a great big rally to seal the deal, or so thought Walker's allies and funders—particularly the billionaire Koch brothers, who paid for that Saturday's event via their generous donations to the group Americans for Prosperity. Buses would roll from across the state. And Palin, the paid spokeswoman for the Tea Party movement, would pull the crowd.

April 16 was supposed to be the day when the zombie idea was revived and the uprising was buried.

But something else altogether happened.

Something Tom Paine anticipated.

Paine wrote when the American revolutionary struggle was supposedly on its last legs, "These are the times that try men's souls. The summer soldier and the sunshine patriot will, in this crisis, shrink from the service of their country; but he that stands by it now, deserves the love and thanks of man and woman."

On that Saturday, in Madison, Wisconsin, there was plenty to be thankful for.

Palin pulled a crowd all right. But not the one she expected.

Walker and the zombie idealists may have had the rogue Alaskan. But Walker's critics had the numbers. Madison's ABC television affiliate reported that night that "pro-union labor supporters surrounded smaller groups of tea party members waiting for former Alaska Gov. Sarah Palin to appear outside the Wisconsin Capitol" while the NBC station announced that "a solid core of Tea Partiers were near the stage, but they were flanked on all sides by union protesters who have dominated protests at the Capitol for months. The Tea Party folks had the microphone, but the crowd had the volume, literally and figuratively."

What happened? Wasn't the Tea Party supposed to be the dynamic political force of the 2010s? Wasn't Palin supposed to be the rock star who rallied conservatives on what she declared to be "the frontlines in the battle for our country"?

When Palin got to the frontlines, she was greeted not with a warm embrace but with a throng of Wisconsinites holding their glorious handmade signs:

GRIZZLIES ARE NOT A NATIVE SPECIES

THE MAD HATTER CALLED . . . HE WANTS HIS TEA PARTY BACK

I CAN SEE STUPID FROM MY CONDO

And WISCONSIN LOVES TINA FEY!—a reference to the comic who famously parodied Palin on NBC's *Saturday Night Live.*

To be clear, there were Palinites present in Madison on the day that the former governor flew in. But what was surprising, in a state where the political climate had become so charged, and where there were (and are) such genuine divisions, was that there were not more of them.

Political fights, be they elections or competing rallies, often come down to debates about numbers. This is not necessarily right, but it is how the game is played. So let's look at the numbers debate from that one day in April—not because they are in and of themselves definitional but because they illustrate some of the challenges and opportunities that exist for a movement that relies more on people power than money power. As the rapid growth of the Occupy Wall Street movement in the fall of 2011 so clearly illustrated, there is a clear desire on the part of the American people to rise up and be heard. But there remains a tendency on the part not just of the media but of political elites to try and impose a "fair and balanced" frame on coverage of competing movements and ideas. This is a frustrating reality, but not one that argues against street-based activism. Rather, it argues for getting serious about numbers and media: for generating real crowds and making sure that the real story is told, even if that means the story must be told by the movement itself. Just as the Populists, the Progressives, the Nonpartisan Leaguers, the Farmer Laborites, and the Socialists of a century ago recognized they would need to create their own media—and their own politics—so will a new generation of radicals.

That truth was self-evident on April 16.

After a week of relatively mild weather, that Saturday came wind-blown and bitter cold with freezing rain turning to snow by the time Palin, wearing designer clothes and a grimace, appeared. Instead of the masses of Tea Partisans that had been predicted, the group the former governor addressed outside the state capitol filled a 20 × 35–foot space between a riser packed with television cameras and a stage area where organizers with money to burn had erected an entirely unnecessary big-screen TV and concert speakers.

Even if the Tea Partisans packed into the space as tightly as possible, they could not have numbered more than six or seven hundred. Local concert promoter Tag Evers, whose years of experience organizing events (including a few anti-Walker rallies) gave him an eye for crowds, put the number of Palin enthusiasts at five hundred. Defending Wisconsin activist Jeremy Ryan announced after rallying against Palin that "there were probably about 500 of them . . . and 5,000 of us. . . . Even when they bus people in from other states, they still can't form a majority."

But let's be generous. Let's say that, with the Tea Partisans who were outside the enclosed and heavily policed area where Palin spoke, the supporters of Governor Walker's agenda numbered one thousand.

That would mean that the Tea Partisans were outnumbered more than five to one by the mass of anti-Walker protesters that surrounded the Palin event, ringing cowbells and shouting, "Shame! Shame! Shame!" as the Alaskan delivered a speech that focused mainly on national issues. (As it turned out, she was being filmed by a friendly crew of moviemakers who had hoped to use the event as an opportunity to highlight the 2008 Republican vice presidential nominee's lingering "appeal.") In her brief references to Wisconsin, Palin offered Orwellian rewrites of reality, such as a claim that "[Walker's] not trying to hurt union members. Hey, folks, he's trying to save your jobs and your pensions."

Though it was organized in only a matter of hours, the protest against Palin and Walker easily overwhelmed the gathering of those who came to support the former Alaska governor and the recall-threatened Wisconsin governor. Police estimated that roughly sixty-five hundred people were on the capitol square that Saturday, and everywhere you looked there were firefighters, police officers, teachers, public employees, farmers, small business owners, and their allies waving signs that read SCOTT—PULL A PALIN—QUIT!

Worried that the media might miss the real story of April 16, Madisonian Bill Bunke said, "I hope the cameras they've got focused on Palin turn around and tell the real story of what happened today."

That was too tall an order, as Palin and the Tea Party continued to enjoy inflated coverage not just from conservative media outlets such as Fox News—the subject of posters car-

ried by union activists that read FOX WILL LIE ABOUT THIS and
ACCORDING TO FOX I'M NOT HERE—but also mainstream national media outlets that presented Palin, a failed vice presidential candidate who resigned her governorship, as a serious
spokesperson for the right.

Despite the media misrepresentations, the crowd that surrounded the Tea Party event knew how things played out that
Saturday on Palin's "frontlines." They were declaring victory
as the Alaskan was jetting out of town. "Who would have
thought that Sarah Palin would give this movement a boost?"
joked Terry Fritter, an American Federation of State, County
and Municipal Employees union member who had attended
most of the anti-Walker rallies at the capitol.

Fritter started his day at a rally on the opposite side of the
capitol from the Palin event. Organized by the Wisconsin Wave
coalition that brought together union, environmental, and
community groups, the rally featured all Wisconsin speakers—
unlike the Tea Party event—and was addressed by newly
elected Madison mayor Paul Soglin, who noted the dramatically larger turnout by union members and their allies.

Soglin was not alone in recognizing the reality of the day.
The energy and volume of the thousands who came to
protest Palin, Walker, and the zombie idea of taking from the
poor and giving to the rich unsettled the speakers at the Tea
Party event. A local conservative talk-radio host shouted from
the stage that union backers should "shut up." Andrew Breitbart, one of many national conservative figures flown in for
the event, told the union members and their allies to "go to
hell."

But while the sunshine patriots huddled near the Palin stage
may have taken some solace from the taunts, the Winter Soldiers were unbothered and unbowed. "They're mad because

we outnumber them," said Fritter. "They're mad because we're not backing down."

Fritter's point is not just accurate, it is instructive. One of the reasons that right-wing politicians and pundits, and their echo chamber in the media, so disrespect and so aggressively dismiss popular protest from Wisconsin to Wall Street is to discourage dissent. It was not uncommon during the course of 2011 to hear protests by middle-class families and prim-and-proper students dismissed as gatherings "of filthy hippies," "criminals" and "union thugs." The truth is quickly sacrificed by those who fear the numbers and the message of protesters against a corrupt status quo. This is unfortunate, but this is not going to change. Terry Fritter's lessons are the right ones to take away from the new wave of dissent and protest: "we outnumber them" and "we're not backing down." In other words, those who would change the system must recognize that they will be dismissed and discouraged in order to get them to back down. The necessary response is not just to refuse to do so but to recognize that the attacks themselves provide the best indication that power is threatened. That is the point at which progressives must redouble their efforts.

This is what Tom Paine taught the rebels of another age. The Wisconsin movement was young on April 16, 2011. The Occupy Wall Street movement did not yet exist. Before the year was done, however, both movements would, through sheer resilience, transform the political debate in the United States—not as separate initiatives but as extensions from one another: Wisconsin inspiring Occupy Wall Street, Occupy Wall Street reinspiring Wisconsin, and the collaboration inspiring a nation. This new movement of the 99 percent of Americans who refuse anymore to stand on the sidelines of American democracy has experienced great successes and frustrating setbacks. More hope and more disappointment will come. So be it. As the pamphleteer noted in "The Crisis," "Tyranny, like hell, is not easily conquered; yet we have this consolation with us, that the harder the conflict, the more glorious the triumph. What we obtain too cheap, we esteem too lightly: it is dearness only that gives every thing its value. Heaven knows how to put a proper price upon its goods; and it would be strange indeed if so celestial an article as FREEDOM should not be highly rated."

★ ★ ★

PAINE SPENT HIS last days in New York City, frequenting the public houses of Lower Manhattan, where the promise of his revolution had been realized not with a military victory or even with a Constitution but with the bending of the elected leaders of the new nation to a popular demand that the Constitution be amended to respect the rights of the people.

It was on the island of Manhattan, not in Philadelphia nor on the swamp that would become Washington, D.C., that the founders of the American experiment gathered at the first Congress of the United States. Their purpose, in those last weeks of September 1789, was to ratify and circulate to the states amendments to the constitution. Those amendments outlined protections against the abuses of the corrupt elites and organized factions that Jefferson, Madison, and their democratic circle feared would eventually grasp control of government, and turn it against the people. It was at No. 26 Wall Street that they spelled out affirmative rights that were imagined as tools for the reclaiming of authority by the people. The most important of these were contained in the First Amendment.

A right to freedom of speech provided an encouragement to speak truth to power, as Americans did when they read their

Declaration of Independence in the town squares and on the country crossroads of the thirteen British colonies that would rise to challenge the crude calculus of empire and imperialism.

A right to freedom of the press urged on the circulation of radical ideas, like those Paine used to call colonials to revolution against the British Empire.

A right to assemble and a right to petition for the redress of grievances.

The right to speak has been battered not just by censors of language and ideas but by a United States Supreme Court majority that, in its deference to Wall Street, has imagined protections for corporate "speech" that permit the CEOs and hedge-fund managers who make up a dominant upper one percent of society to shout down the individual voices (and votes) of the great mass of Americans who make up a lower 99 percent that is increasingly disempowered economically and politically.

Consolidation of media ownership, the replacement of the historic civic and democratic values of independent media with the commercial and entertainment values of contemporary corporate media, the threats to the diversity and the promise of the Internet posed by attacks on net neutrality, have all conspired to reframe the guarantee of freedom of the press as a protection for billionaire media moguls such as Rupert Murdoch.

This would not have surprised Jefferson or Madison, whose writings regularly pondered just such threats.

That is why they trusted in the most essential of freedoms, the rights to assemble and petition for the redress of grievances—the very rights that the crowds in Wisconsin exercised in February and March of 2011. The very rights that, on the 222nd anniversary of the ratification of the First Amendment, students and unemployed young adults and a growing number

of their elders were exercising at Zuccotti Park in Lower Manhattan as part of the Occupy Wall Street movement.

As it was in Madison, the Occupy Wall Street activists were
accused of reflexively objecting rather than offering concrete
demands, even though their advocacy for a fair and equitable
society was far more credible than the failed fantasy that the
United States could ever be renewed by rapacious capitalism.

As it was in Madison, those who rejected the zombie ideal
that the rich must get richer, the poor must get poorer, and
the middle class must wither away, were dismissed by conservative commentators as an insufficiently patriotic rabble. Rush
Limbaugh decried the Occupy Wall Street movement as a
crowd of "anarchists" and "union thugs," echoing the language
he had just a few months earlier used to attack the Wisconsin
demonstrators. Herman Cain, a millionaire bidder for the Tea
Party affections once wasted on Sarah Palin, condemned Occupy Wall Street as "un-American."

But as I surveyed the occupying masses on a mild fall
evening, I felt the same sense as I had on those cold winter
nights in Madison. The spirit of resistance not just to political
power but to the corporations that pull the puppet strings of
our politicians, the reoccupation of public space that had been
co-opted by the elites, the reassertion of rights that had lan-
guished for too long: all of this and more provided an outline
for a new politics of protest.

These were Americans, acting as the best of the founders
had expected they would. Their demand was rooted not in
some foreign premise but in Paine's principle that "when it
shall be said in any country in the world my poor are happy;
neither ignorance nor distress is to be found among them; my
jails are empty of prisoners, my streets of beggars; the aged are
not in want; the taxes are not oppressive; the rational world is

my friend, because I am a friend of its happiness: When these things can be said, then may that country boast of its Constitution and its Government."

This was not something new. This was a coming home to that which was known, but almost forgotten.

The process of perfecting this country's Constitution and its government began on the island of Manhattan.

The Bill of Rights was submitted for ratification at No. 26 Wall Street.

The Occupy Wall Street movement had come home to the birthplace of our Bill of Rights. And it was using the most essential rights, to assemble, to petition for the redress of grievances, to assert anew, as James Madison did during those deliberations at No. 26 Wall Street, "that the people have an indubitable, unalienable, and indefeasible right to reform or change their Government, whenever it be found adverse or inadequate to the purposes of its institution."

The defenders of elite power, of empire and authoritarianism, the Tories of a new age would continue to claim that the protests that spread from New York to Des Moines, to Topeka, to Denver, to Portland were unpatriotic—just as they had decried the Madison protests that outlined so many of the themes and tactics of the Occupy Wall Street movement.

But the Tories were wrong.

The new protest movements of 2011, of 2012, and beyond are the most patriotic thing to come out of the precincts around Wall Street in 222 years.

"The shortest and most effectual remedy is to begin anew," wrote Paine in *The Rights of Man*.

America began with an uprising. And, now, in a city named for the essential author of the Constitution, on the streets where the Bill of Rights was forged and ratified, on college campuses and in union halls, in small towns and on capitol squares, the American uprising is beginning anew.

Let us proceed as Paine hoped we would, believing once more that "we have every opportunity and every encouragement before us, to form the noblest, purest constitution on the face of the earth. We have it in our power to begin the world over again. A situation, similar to the present, hath not happened since the days of Noah until now. The birthday of a new world is at hand."

SOURCE NOTES

As a political writer for the *Nation* magazine and an editor of the *Capital Times* newspaper in Madison, Wisconsin, I covered the uprising in Wisconsin from day one. But long before the opening of the specific struggle detailed in this book, I was writing for these publications and others about the issues that are the focus of its chapters.

While this book amplifies and extends beyond what appeared in the *Nation* and the *Capital Times*, the news articles and essays I did for both provide a detailed outline of the reporting I did on the struggle in Wisconsin and related national struggles.

The *Nation*'s online archives, at http://www.thenation .com/blogs/john-nichols, contain my reporting and essays about Wisconsin.

On March 3, 2011, the *Nation* carried my initial cover story on the struggle, "The Spirit of Wisconsin." Other cover stories on Wisconsin and the struggles in the states include "Showdown in Wisconsin" (March 10, 2011), "The Post-Wisconsin Game Plan" (May 11, 2011), and "The Democrats' Rural Rebellions" (August 23, 2011). An early cover story I wrote on "Occupy Wall Street" appeared October 12, 2011, as "The 99 Percent Rise Up." Another piece, "OWS to Super Committee: Accountability, Not Austerity," appeared on October 19, 2011.

My writing for the *Capital Times* about Wisconsin and the struggles in the states, as well as the Occupy Wall Street phenomenon, can be found at www.madison.com. The *Capital Times* articles provide particularly detailed coverage of the recall campaigns and electoral fights related to the Wisconsin uprising.

In addition to my articles and columns for the *Nation* and the *Capital Times*, the *Progressive*, a national publication based in Madison for which I have written for more than a decade, published a cover story, "The Wisconsin Model," in the July 2011 issue. And the *Guardian* published a piece, "Wisconsin: Crucible for a New American Left," on March 18, 2011, which began to outline the broader analysis contained in this book.

Here are some notes on the specific chapters:

FOREWORD

Rebecca Solnit's "Acts of Hope: Challenging Empire on the World Stage" appeared in the January/February 2004 edition of *Orion* magazine. Bill O'Reilly's Fox News report on the palm trees appeared on the evening of March 1, 2011.

Media Matters for America did an analysis of the Fox coverage of the Wisconsin protests, "'Fox News Lies' While Covering Pro-Labor Protests in Wisconsin," which appeared March 2, 2011, and can be found online at www.mediamatters.org.

I've written a good deal over the years about my roots in Wisconsin. One of the more extensive pieces, "Portrait of the Founder: Fighting Bob La Follette," appeared in the January 1999 issue of the *Progressive*.

CHAPTER I:
"MADISON, WISCONSIN, LET'S GET ROWDY!"

Readers can delve into the details of the governor's plan at his official website: walker.wi.gov. The key release is headlined "Governor Walker Introduces Budget Repair: Emergency measure is needed to balance the state budget and give government the tools to manage during economic crisis." The governor regularly made statements on the fight, all of which are archived at http://walker.wi.gov/mediaroom.asp?locid =177.

Tom Morello wrote about his experiences in Madison for *Rolling Stone* magazine. The article, "Frostbite and Freedom: Tom Morello on the Battle of Madison," appeared February 25, 2011. *Rolling Stone* also featured a fine article on Morello's visit, "Tom Morello Rages Against Anti-Union Bill at Wisconsin Rally: 'This legislation would rob us of decades, centuries of social progress,' Morello said," which appeared February 22, 2011, on www.rollingstone.com. It was penned by Patrick Doyle.

An interview I did with Morello, "Guitars and Bagpipes: Tom Morello's Justice Tour Links Rockers and Unions for a Labor Day Fightback," appeared September 4, 2011, at www.thenation.com.

Morello's website is at www.nightwatchmanmusic.com. It features a fine archive of articles and videos from his Wisconsin visits and his appearances at Occupy Wall Street events.

The Street Dogs' website is at www.streetdogs. com. It features video of the group performing in Madison.

Claude Lévi-Strauss's *Tristes Tropiques* was first published in 1955. A solid contemporary edition is published in paperback by Penguin. I was introduced to Lévi-Strauss's wise assessment of the world by my friend Alexander Cockburn. I remain eternally grateful to both of them. Patrick Wilcken wrote a decent biography of Lévi-Strauss, *The Poet in His Laboratory* (Penguin Press), which appeared in 2010. Of *Tristes Tropiques* Wilcken writes, "In a world of ever more specialized areas of knowledge, there may never again be a body of work of such exhilarating reach and ambition."

CHAPTER 2:

FIRST AMENDMENT REMEDIES

There are many fine biographies of James Madison, including several that I relied upon in writing this chapter, including Ralph Ketcham's *James Madison: A Biography* (University of Virginia Press, 1990), Garry Wills's *James Madison* (Times Books, 2002), and Andrew Burstein's *Madison and Jefferson* (Random House, 2010).

Madison's own writings on the Constitution are well collected and archived by the Avalon Project at the Yale Law School's Lillian Goldman Law Library. The project can be accessed online at http://avalon.law.yale.edu/subject_menus/debcont.asp.

I have written extensively about the founding convention in several recent books, including *The Genius of Impeachment: The Founders' Cure for Royalism* (New Press, 2006). I have for many years written about the battle between right and left over how to interpret the Constitution, in articles such as "The Tea Party Constitution versus the Thomas Jefferson Constitution" (*Nation*, October 30, 2010) and "Tea Partisans Misread the Constitution" (*Capital Times*, January 9, 2011).

Robert M. La Follette's autobiography remains a rich resource. A good edition is *La Follette's Autobiography: A Personal*

Narrative of Political Experiences (University of Wisconsin Press, 1960.) Nancy Unger's biography of the legendary governor and senator, *Fighting Bob La Follette: The Righteous Reformer* (University of North Carolina Press, 2000) provides terrific detail and perspective.

Michele Bachmann's dismissal of the Wisconsin protests were featured on Fox News, February 18, 2011. Rush Limbaugh's comments on Wisconsin are archived at "Union Thugs Turn Wisconsin into Greece as Freeloaders Protest" at www.rushlimbaugh.com.

Ann Coulter's *Demonic: How the Liberal Mob Is Endangering America* (Crown, 2011) outlined her theories about the dangers of mass protest and the Wisconsin uprising. She expounded on these theories in numerous interviews, including a detailed interview on Fox News with Sean Hannity, which aired March 10, 2011.

Sharon Angle's "Second Amendment solutions" comment came in an interview with conservative talk-radio host Lars Larson, and is detailed in Greg Sargent's Plum Line article "Sharon Angle Floated Possibility of Armed Insurrection" (*Washington Post*, June 15, 2010).

CHAPTER 3:
THE ARC OF HISTORY BENDS TOWARD SOLIDARITY

Howard Zinn, a friend and mentor, gave us our radical history back. *A People's History of the United States: 1492–Present* (Harper Perennial, 2003) is his essential work, but I rely also on his fine autobiography, *You Can't Be Neutral on a Moving Train: A Personal History of Our Times* (Beacon; 2002). Rebecca Solnit's comment on how revolutions linger appeared in an article, "Hope and Turmoil in 2011," which she wrote March 20, 2011,

and which appeared at www.thenation.com and at www.
tomdispatch.com.

Most of this chapter is based on reporting on the ground
in Madison and around Wisconsin, as well as on interviews
and conversations with activists nationwide. I am indebted to
the Murphy Institute at the City University of New York for
inviting me to their May 13, 2011, forum on labor and state-
based struggles, which prodded me to consider lessons for how
best to emulate Wisconsin. I also appreciate the collaboration
with the *Progressive*'s Matt Rothschild, which led to the cover
story "The Wisconsin Model" (*Progressive*, July 2011). Matt's
encouragement led me to explore the radical traditions of various states, which are outlined and mentioned in this chapter.

Much has been written comparing the Wisconsin and Occupy Wall Street movements. I think there is a connection, but
there are differences as well. Andy Kroll, writing for *Mother
Jones* on October 6, 2011, produced what I think is an especially strong compare-and-contrast analysis: "From Wisconsin
to Wall Street, An Economic Reckoning." When I visited the
Occupy Wall Street encampment in New York, I had many
good discussions with folks on the ground, especially Jeff
Smith, about these issues. They helped to shape my thinking.

For details regarding Fighting Bob Fest, visit the sites
www.fightingbobfest.org and www.fightingbob.com, both of
which benefit from the insights of the wise and good Ed Garvey. The best biography of Gaylord Nelson is *The Man from
Clear Lake* (University of Wisconsin Press, 2004) by Bill
Christofferson, an able political strategist and thinker who was
very much a part of the Wisconsin struggle. I knew and interviewed Gaylord many times. In writing this chapter, and
thinking about his role in Wisconsin history, I also benefitted
from conversations with Gaylord's daughter, Tia Nelson.

The great anti-corporate jurist Edward Ryan is recalled on the Wisconsin Court System's archive of Supreme Court chief justices at www.wicourts.gov.

CHAPTER 4:
"WISCONSIN IS NOT BROKE,
AMERICA IS NOT BROKE"

Howard Zinn's *A Power Governments Cannot Suppress* was published by City Lights in 2006.

Michael Moore wrote a terrific article on his visit, "How I Got to Madison, Wisconsin," which appeared March 6, 2011, on www.michaelmoore.com, as did the text of the speech he delivered in Madison, as it was written, appears.

Laura Flanders's interview with Michael Moore appeared on GRITtv March 1, 2011.

The website of The Buffalo Beast, Ian Murphy, can be found at www.buffalobeast.com.

The DVD version of Moore's *Capitalism: A Love Story* was released in 2009.

The Wisconsin Legislative Fiscal Bureau's assessments of state budget issues can be found at http://legis.wisconsin .gov/lfb/.

Wisconsin state representative Mark Pocan is the former cochair of the Legislative Joint Finance Committee. His assessments of the Fiscal Bureau's reports and budget issues can be found at http://markpocanwi.blogspot.com/. *Capital Times* coverage of the budget issues included an important analysis, "State's Crisis Political, Not Financial," which appeared February 23, 2011. Another good piece, "Is the State Budget Really in Crisis? Depends Who You Ask," was written by Dee Hall and appeared in the *Wisconsin State Journal*, February 19, 2011.

National Nurses United (NNU) executive director Rose Ann DeMoro and NNU director of public policy Michael Lighty outlined the union's "Tax Wall Street" agenda in a series of interviews and conversations with the author. The NNU's programs and statements are outlined at their website, www.nationalnursesunited.org.

CHAPTER 5: THE NEXT MEDIA SYSTEM

Tom Paine's writings, as quoted in this book, come from *Thomas Paine: Collected Writings—Common Sense, The Crisis, Rights of Man, The Age of Reason, Pamphlets, Articles, and Letters* (Library of America, 1995). It was edited by the brilliant Eric Foner. I have written extensively about Paine and media, most recently in the paperback edition of *The Death and Life of American Journalism* (Nation Books, 2011), which I coauthored with Robert M. McChesney.

Gil Scott-Heron's "Small Talk at 125th and Lenox" was reissued in 1995 by RCA. The piece I wrote on Scott-Heron's passing is archived as "Gil Scott-Heron's Revolution," at www.thenation.com.

To visit archives of MSNBC's *The Ed Show*, go to www.ed.msnbc.com.

To visit archives of *Democracy Now!* go to www.democracynow.org.

To visit archives of *New York Times* coverage, go to www.nytimes.com.

The transcript of Scott Walker's conversation with a caller he thought was David Koch can be found at the website of the group One Wisconsin Now: www.onewisconsinnow.org.

Media Matters of America, which did quite a bit of fine analysis of the coverage of the Wisconsin struggle, is on the web at www.mediamatters.org, while Talking Points Memo is at www.talkingpointsmemo.com.

The Center for Media and Democracy coverage of Wisconsin is archived at the organization's prwatch.org site, and Matt Wisniewski's protest videos are at www.matthew wisniewski.com.

Time magazine's interview with Wisniewski appeared February 22, 2011.

Scott Goodstein and I did our debrief regarding coverage of the Wisconsin struggle and state-based fights in 2011 at the International Labor Communications (ILCA) Association conference, which was held in Seattle in late September. Visit ILCA at www.ilcaonline.org.

CHAPTER 6:

THE RISE OF THE HOUSE OF LABOR

The Debs quote is from an article "The Ideal Labor Press," which appeared in the May 1904 edition of the *Metal Worker* magazine, the Bridges quote comes from a statement made in the mid-1930s, at the time he was leading longshore workers out of the American Federation of Labor and into the Congress of Industrial Organization. There are a number of fine books on Bridges and the International Longshore and Warehouse Union, including Charles P. Larrowe's *Harry Bridges: The Rise and Fall of Radical Labor in the United States* (Lawrence Hill & Co., 1977); and I highly recommend the Harry Bridges Project website at www.theharrybridgesproject.org.

Tom Geoghegan's *Which Side Are You On? Trying to Be for Labor When It's Flat on Its Back*, originally published in 1991, was republished in 2004 by the New Press. It is a brilliant book, well and wisely updated by Geoghegan.

SOURCE NOTES

The South Central Federation of Labor's statement on a general strike can be found at www.scfl.org, as can good background information on general strikes. Erik Loomis wrote a fine essay on general strikes, "Shutting It All Down: The Power of General Strikes in U.S. History," which appeared November 2, 2011, at the *In These Times* website: www.inthesetimes.com. (With writers like David Moberg and Roger Bybee, *In These Times* remains an outstanding source of labor coverage. Mike Elk, a fine young labor reporter, has been contributing to *In These Times* of late, as well.)

The Seattle protests against the WTO in 1999 are an important reference point for the Wisconsin struggle and this book. I covered those protests for the *Nation.* I have relied for information and insight on the WTO History Project, a joint effort of several programs at the University of Washington: the Harry Bridges Center for Labor Studies, the Center for Communication and Civic Engagement, the Digital Initiatives project, and the Manuscripts, Special Collections, and University Archives (MSCUA) division of the university Libraries.

For more on the ALEC Exposed project, visit the Center for Media and Democracy's www.alecexposed.org website. The *Nation's* special issue on ALEC appeared August 1–8, 2011, and was edited by Liliana Segura.

For a good history of the Wisconsin Progressives and Roosevelt, consider Philip La Follette's *Adventure in Politics: The Memoirs of Philip La Follette* (Holt, Rinehart and Winston, 1970). Jonathan Kasparek's *Fighting Son: A Biography of Philip La Follette* (Wisconsin Historical Society; 2006) is also a fine resource. More needs to be written on this era and the state-based third parties of the left, especially the Wisconsin Progressives, the Minnesota Farmer-Labor Party, the New York American Labor Party, and the North Dakota Nonpartisan

176

League. Roosevelt's speech, delivered August 9, 1934, in Green Bay, Wisconsin, can be found on the website of the American Presidency Project, at http://www.presidency.ucsb.edu/.

AFTERWORD:

THE REMEDY IS TO BEGIN ANEW

Paine's "Public Good" can be found in *Thomas Paine: Collected Writings* (Library of America, 1995), which is the source for other Paine quotes in this section. For more on Paine, consider Eric Foner's fine biography, *Tom Paine and Revolutionary America*, republished by Oxford University Press in a fine 2004 edition.

Sarah Palin's visit to Madison is actually immortalized in a bizarre biographical film, *The Undefeated*, which was issued in the summer of 2011. A better take on the event can be found in the coverage by Susie Madrak at www.crooksandliars.com, which features a fine assessment of what happened and some telling videos. Jeremy Ryan's "500 of Them, 5000 of Us!! THIS IS WHAT DEMOCRACY LOOKS LIKE!!?" was featured at www.defendingwisconsin.org.

The Occupy Wall Street movement developed as I was writing this book. I wrote extensively about it for the *Nation* and commented on it for television and radio programs in the United States and abroad. I commend the www.occupywallstr.org website to readers, along with the *Occupied Wall Street Journal*. I visited Occupy Wall Street with Naomi Klein, whose remarks were published in the *Nation*, October 6, 2011, as "Occupy Wall Street: The Most Important Thing in the World Now." Naomi summed things up very well.

And so, of course, did Mr. Paine. We do, indeed, have it in our power to begin the world over again.

INDEX